ALTER YOUR LIFE

ALTER YOUR LIFE

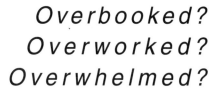

Overbooked?
Overworked?
Overwhelmed?

Dr. Kathleen Hall

Oak Haven
Clarkesville, Georgia

Published by
Oak Haven
P.O. Box 1150
Clarkesville, Georgia 30523

ISBN 0-9745427-2-5

Library of Congress Control Number 2005922034

Cover and Interior Design by George Foster
Typesetting by Desktop Miracles, Inc.

Contents

Acknowledgements

BLESSING IS THE WORD that best describes the process of writing this book. The fabric of my life has been woven together with wise and loving teachers, gifted healers, friends and family. Thank you all for sharing this journey.

Thank you Cynthia Cohen. You came into my life as a guiding light that has led me on an adventure greater than I had imagined. Your searing insight, focus, persistence and love made this book possible. You are my "shero" and my friend.

Thank you Rick Roberts, who inspired me to write this particular book for Harriet. Your seasoned skill challenged me and helped me flesh out the book and gave me the sacred gift of Harriet.

Thank you Donna Godzisz. You are my angel of God. You are my confidant, an ingenious source of wisdom and love along with being my literary assistant. You are my friend who spent innumerable hours typing and sharing egg and cheese sandwiches as we wrote while watching the sun rise at Waffle House. Your energy, loyalty and dedication continually inspires and encourages me.

Carol Ann White, thank you for your contribution to my original manuscript.

I am especially grateful to Willy Spizman and Jenny Corsey of the Spizman Agency, who have contributed greatly to the completion of this project.

Thank you to my friends and soul sisters. Pamela Hayling Hoffman, my constant source of love, loyalty, and encouragement. I love you. Donna Andrews, a gift of support and guidance in many hours of darkness. I love you.

Jean Dye, Susie Levan, Joyce Newman, and Helen Maddox—you are my friends and my inspiration. I love you.

Thank you to my team at Alter Your Life; you are the wind beneath my wings. We are family—I love you.

Thank you to the people who have believed in my dream and blessed me with resources to make it come true. A special thanks to you, my friend, David Stovall.

Thank you to my spiritual teachers and mentors, who are too many to name you all. To name a few, Dr. Bill Mallard, Dr. Roberta Bondi, Dr. Sally Purvis, Dr. John Kloepfer, President Jimmy Carter, Bishop Desmond Tutu, Arun Gandhi, the Dalai Lama, Thich Nhat Hanh, Wong Loh Sin See, and all the saints of the Church who constantly inspire me and give me courage.

Thank you to the gifted healers that have helped heal my heart and soul, Dr. Pat Malone, Dr. Carol Holzhalb, and Wendy Palmer Patterson.

Thank you to my beautiful mother, Mary Lee Clennan who has a voice like an angel, who taught me to laugh, dream, listen to my inner voice, write, and love.

Thank you to my father, Dale F. Hall, who taught me the value of hard work, forgiveness, and the infinite possibilities created when you take risks.

Thank you to my family—Jon, Jeffrey, Pamela, Patricia, Candice, and Will—for our difficult lives fraught with suffering, joy and hope. There's light at the end of the tunnel.

Thank you Pat Walsh, Capitol Area Mosaic and my kids who taught me about real economic poverty, spiritual wealth and that infinite possibilities are everywhere.

Thank you to Oak Haven—my farm, my Avalon, my Camelot, my Walden Pond all in one. Thank you to the animals that have been my most profound teachers. Thank you Secret, Reba, Shadow and all of the sacred horses that have taught me invaluable lessons about power, death, fear and mothering. I shall be eternally grateful—I love you.

I love you Lady, Holly, Lucy, and Abbey, my angel dogs who are now with the angels. Thank you to all of my dogs for teaching me about love, playfulness, loyalty and wisdom.

A special thank you to my dog Chloe for never leaving my side through my depression, my dissertation, writing this book, and life.

Thank you JC Cowart. You have been a constant source of strength. You are a dying breed of cowboy and farmer. You have been my great teacher about the land, animals, the weather and life.

Thank you to my patients and clients who have been my teachers, mentors and family. A special thank you to the Cardiac-Pulmonary Wellness Group: Shirlene, Dick, Ilone, Nancy, Gail, Wally, Helen, Jane, Lucille, Catherine, Roy, Emily, and you unnamed, but you know who you are. I love you and am eternally grateful.

Thank you my children Brittany and Elizabeth. Brittany, you have always been a source of healing for me, many years before you became a physician. You live and breathe compassion, forgiveness and love. Elizabeth, you have always been a source of passionate love, intuition and creativity. You have been my mirror, my darling, and I am eternally grateful. If I have contributed anything to the healing of this planet in my life, I believe it is the gift of these two children.

Thank you my darling Jim, for over 30 years you have been my partner, cheerleader, advisor, and lover. Very few have committed the time and passion to be an amazing husband and father. You have always believed in me. I loved you the first moment I looked into your eyes at the Medical Center and I always will.

I am grateful Holy One—Divine Presence, Light, God, Creator of all life—I live every moment aware of your presence, guidance, and love. I live my life to be one with you in the sacred process of co-creation.

The Invitation

THE THEMES THAT RULE OUR LIVES TODAY ARE, "I just don't have time" and "I'm exhausted." We are overbooked, overworked and overwhelmed. Just getting done what must be done fills our days. The notion of finding a precious hour or two to learn how to create balance, reduce our stress and discover an intentional life to soothe our aching souls is simply out of the question. This book provides an alternative to the struggle to "make time" for renewal.

I found out years ago, when I worked as a financial advisor with a Wall Street firm at the World Trade Center, that my next promotion wasn't going to make me any happier. A newer Mercedes wouldn't fill what was missing in my life. In fact, research has shown that the wealthy are no happier than those without a lot of money. They are no more satisfied, no more content and no more at peace with their lives, the people around them, or themselves.

The demands of our time never seem to end. Our jobs need us, our children need us, and, increasingly, our aging parents need us. We don't get enough sleep, we eat too many meals on the run, we take too many pills and we don't spend enough time with our children and the people we love.

Stress is "The Epidemic of the 21st Century." We now have scientific evidence that chronic stress shortens our lives, accelerates the aging process, and is a direct contributor to cancer, heart disease, obesity, hypertension, arthritis, diabetes and too many other diseases to name. Our current research reveals that the medical toll of chronic stress costs Americans at least $300 billion a year in treatment and lost productivity.

So what can we do?

We can discover how to live an intentional life in a manner that requires no doctrine, no memorization of a new vocabulary, no trekking off to distant holy lands. It does not require us to change our jobs, our lifestyle or transplant our personalities. It doesn't even require any additional time. Sound too good to be true?

We simply make a subtle internal shift that brings greater and greater rewards with practice. We can begin by listening to our authentic self and living our lives "from the inside out" instead of struggling to control the ever-changing chaos around us. We can learn to shift from *making* things happen to *allowing* them to unfold naturally. The acorn does not push, does not "try harder," but simply knows that it is an oak tree and trusts the wisdom of its life process.

We can develop our own unique personal practices that can help us return "home" once we realize that we are out of balance. In time these practices will become an effortless and restorative part of living an intentional life of mental, physical and spiritual well being.

Most of us aren't even aware we are not living an intentional life. We have lived our entire lives reacting to whatever life throws at us. We haven't realized the power of our thoughts, our desires and our intentions. This is difficult for many of us to understand because society doesn't even teach this simple truth, and our institutions and cultural traditions don't reveal it. Living an intentional life is listening to our lives and understanding at a very profound level that our lives are the product of our choices.

There are three ingredients, or components that are the foundation for living an intentional life. They are *awareness, choice,* and *energy*, which is easy to remember as *ACE*. These essential roots for living an intentional life are not sequential. The key is to become aware of these three key elements in your life and learn how to navigate them.

The process can begin by developing your *awareness* (A) of the daily experiences of your life. I advise each client and patient to pay attention and "listen to your life." Listen to what ignites your passion and creativity, to what gives you energy. Listen to what drains you, distracts you, and irritates you. These are the first clues to becoming more conscious of the nature of the life you now live, the one you have already created.

This awareness leads to a desire to exercise intentional *choice* (C) in your life. Once you are aware that your life is the result of a series of your choices, and the life you are currently living is a result of the choices you have already made, you learn to take responsibility for your life. Victim mentality ends when you understand the power of choice. You may not control many of the circumstances in your life, but you can choose your attitude and intentions in response to circumstances.

Developing your awareness and making intentional choices creates new *energy* (E) and power in your life. When you begin listening to your life, you become more aware of what you are eating, who you are living with, and where you go to work each day. You will begin to notice an energy swelling within you as you become more aware. If you choose to stay in a challenging job or relationship, you can choose to change your attitude. You will make new and different choices, because you now know that life is your choice, and you are the hero of your life, not the victim. You will radiate confidence and a new sense of your own power. As you follow this energy, you will be lead down the path to your intentional life. Your energy fuels your passion and as a result you experience the joy of living an intentional life.

Awareness, choice, and *energy* (ACE) are not experienced in any particular order. Once you understand each component, you will see that they are woven into the fabric of living an intentional life. You may wake up one day and have no *energy* or passion. You may feel "out of gas." You may be watching a movie or reading a novel, and one of the characters creates a profound sadness within you, and suddenly you become *aware* that the life you are living feels shallow, lonely and fearful, and that you miss the *energy* of feeling truly alive. There may be an accident or event in your life that wakes you up and you become *aware* that your life must change, and a *choice* must be made.

As you live an intentional life, you begin to grow inward and downward, rooting yourself deeply into a healthy, fulfilling, abundant life. You are able to achieve a deeper understanding of the simple, the mundane and the ordinary moments, which bring real happiness, inner balance and fulfillment.

Living an intentional life redefines our common notion of "success" by creating depth, meaning and purpose in our lives. True success is based on self-knowledge, balance, freedom and connection, whereas success today is often erroneously seen as the collection of wealth, beauty, or power. In a society driven by a pop culture with lofty benchmarks of athletic prowess, beauty and accumulation of wealth, we must ask ourselves: How happy are we really? How many *happy* people, including yourself, do you really know?

By happiness I mean experiencing a meaningful and intentional life. What is missing in your life is not more stuff, or a new diet, or any form of physical accumulation. What is missing for many of us is the ability to see life in terms of meaning, balance and fulfillment. This book creates a path for you to discover how to live an intentional life infused with meaning and joy in your everyday activities and responsibilities.

One of the crucial benefits of living an intentional life is achieving work-life balance. The real secret of work-life balance is knowing you have choices in all events, experiences and people in your life.

Simply knowing you have choice restores your power.

As we practice awareness, moment by moment, we can gather information about what moves us away from our true self, creating dissatisfaction and anxiety. And we can discover what moves us toward our true self, nourishing us, bringing us a strong sense of satisfaction, purpose and power.

This book offers tools to help you find your own unique choices that will bring greater balance to your demanding life. These simple effective tools, based on age-old, time-honored medical, psychological and spiritual knowledge and wisdom, will soon become second nature and bring with them a greater sense of ease and fulfillment.

The great religious and spiritual traditions have always suggested that the most meaningful and powerful moments of our lives are available in the common, ordinary, mundane tasks of living. Discovering these precious moments for yourself is the point of this book. It simply begins by seeing the world not just in terms of physical activity and visible results, but also in terms of emotional, mental, and spiritual fulfillment. You have the capacity to "re-vision" your life, and this book is a guide to developing that capacity. *Awareness, choice,* and *energy* are available to you every day. Practicing them is easy, and, remarkably, their very smallness and simplicity hold the promise for major transformation in your life.

You can learn how to ride at the center of your life, just as when you were young, you learned to ride a bicycle. And, just like riding a bicycle, once you master the principles of work-life balance, you are on the path to living an intentional life.

You can develop your own unique practices that will allow you to explore your magnificent life in every aspect of your existence. The task is simple; the task is at hand. The rewards are extraordinary.

Let's begin.

AWARENESS

Discovering the Extraordinary in the Ordinary

A Bathroom

O**N A COLD NIGHT IN 1994,** I cleaned the girl's bathroom at North Atlanta High School.

It wasn't something I had planned to do.

It had been an unusually busy day for me. I was racing from a business meeting to get to my daughter's basketball playoff game that evening. It was dinnertime and I had worked through lunch. I was exhausted, hungry, and very late. As I flew up into the stands, a buzzer rang, signaling the end of the first quarter. My daughter had already scored eight points and the game was tied. I sat down by my husband, but immediately realized I just had to go to the bathroom before the game started again. I jumped up, kissed him, and told him I'd be right back.

I raced down the bleachers with my high heels clacking and my cashmere coat falling from my shoulders. I only had a few minutes to get to the women's room and back to watch one of the last basketball games of my daughter's high school career. She was a senior and quite an accomplished guard.

Preoccupied, as my day continued to swirl in my mind, I threw open the bathroom door and rushed in, only to be stopped in my tracks. It was like being hit between the eyes. Before me stood one of the most disgusting scenes I had ever encountered. The sinks were filled with used paper towels, hair, toilet paper, and pooled brown water. The floors were covered with used toilet paper; used sanitary pads and tampons had been thrown around everywhere. The toilets had not been flushed in who knows how long, and were filled with excrement. The mirrors were smattered with obscene graffiti. The restroom was awash in filth, reeking of urine, feces, and old blood. The smell was so bad I gagged.

It was a scene that is still disturbingly clear in my memory.

Rage followed my initial moments of disgust. I was indignant and appalled and filled with judgment. My thoughts went something like this: *Look at how low human nature can go. It's disgusting for any human being to sink to this level of decadence—let alone in my daughter's school. A public school cannot look like this. Who allows it? This is simply uncivilized. Worse, I cannot believe that I allow my children to go to a school like this.*

Then an even darker side of myself crept in. *This is what happens when people don't have anything, I thought. This is what happens when people who have nothing come into a beautiful facility like this. They destroy it. They trash it and have no respect for this school or for themselves.*

In that exact moment, at the height of my rage, as my heart was racing and my blood pressure was pounding, when the anguish and judgment were most monumental, I just stopped. I stood silent as a certain weird shift in my awareness took over my mind. I realized everything I thought and felt was wrong.

My thoughts stopped, my breathing slowed down. A profound still presence overcame me. My intense collection of rash emotions, smells and visual images in this bathroom jogged my memory, and I thought of the story of another bathroom told to me by my friend Arun Gandhi, the grandson of Mahatma Gandhi. The story was used in a scene in the movie about Gandhi's life.

In this scene, Mahatma Gandhi was firmly scolding his wife for not wanting to clean the latrines when it was her turn on the schedule at an ashram in Durban, South Africa. Gandhi's wife thought it was beneath her to clean the latrines, even though everyone that lived at the ashram had to take their turn at every task.

Gandhi believed that full participation by every human, no matter what their status, deepened compassion, humility and connection to every living being. He taught it was fundamental to the true progress of humankind that the most mundane and common activities be shared by all persons equally. Gandhi felt that these simple everyday tasks, common to all of our lives, provided essential—and often surprisingly powerful—lessons on our life journey. These principles were foundational to living an intentional life.

Suddenly, Gandhi and his philosophical ideals were no longer just words on a page, an image on a screen or a story told by his grandson. It was as though Gandhi was in that high school bathroom with me. It was a "perfect storm" moment for me. In that moment all my study, experiences and training about awareness, choice, forgiveness, compassion and service were being played out on this stage of my life in an extraordinary way. In that moment of awareness, I realized I had an incredibly powerful choice to make.

I closed my eyes and asked my teacher Gandhi, if somehow, in some small way, I would be transformed by this experiment with surrender and choice.

I saw the cleaning closet on my left. I walked over to it, opened the door, and found the cleaning supplies stored inside. I took off my coat and hung it on the closet door. I rolled up the sleeves to my suit, took a deep breath, and prayed that I could make it through this experience. I prayed to be made better in some way because of it. I started with the floors. As I cleaned up each piece of disgusting trash, I prayed for compassion and understanding. As I cleaned each sink, I prayed for non-judgment and serenity. As I began on the toilets, I prayed to stay centered and strong, as the stench enveloped me.

I practiced staying in the present moment so I would not get overwhelmed. Eventually I looked up and the bathroom sparkled.

As I closed the supply closet and picked up my coat, I felt like a very different person than the person who entered that bathroom a short time earlier. I learned that my judgment and anger could have separated me from an experience that transformed my life. I discovered that a bathroom filled with the filth of others was a classroom for me. There are people whose job it is to clean bathrooms every day, and I now have a better understanding of these individuals and a great reverence for their courage, perseverance and humility.

I walked back up to my husband in the bleachers and sat down. He thought I had been at the concession stand, or perhaps talking to another parent. I just nodded, smiled, and said nothing.

In the second half of the game, my husband leaned over to me and whispered in my ear, "Honey, I smell Clorox. It's strong. Can you smell it, too?" I smiled and answered, "Yes, dear." I said a silent prayer of thanks to Mahatma Gandhi for opening one of many doors that would transform my life.

A Dog

I was with my younger daughter one evening on the way to the grocery store. Out of nowhere, a large object appeared in the middle of the road. I slammed on my brakes. As the car slid sideways, I tried to make out what was in the road. As we finally came to a stop, I realized it was a dog, apparently it had been hit by a car and left behind.

I have had a practice for many years now of always stopping when there are dead animals on a road, moving them back to the side of the road, and giving them back to the earth. I do this as an act of reverent respect for all creatures. It continually reminds me that these creatures are sacred and I am responsible for their care and protection. I cannot stand the thought of a dead animal being disrespectfully hit again and again by automobiles.

As traffic whizzed by, I was afraid that other cars would hit the dog. I turned the car around, drove beside the dog, stopped, and put on my emergency flashers. The poor dog was dead yet still so precious. I grabbed her two back legs and gently dragged her off to the side of the road. I then pulled her over to the grassy area and squatted down beside her.

I took a deep breath and looked back to the car as my daughter sat gazing out the window at me. After saying a prayer over the dog, I returned to the car, opened the trunk, pulled out some paper towels, and cleaned off my hands. I got in the car and we drove off in hushed silence toward the grocery store.

A few minutes later, the silence was broken. My daughter reached over and tenderly laid her hand over my hand on the gearshift. She looked at me with teary eyes and said, "You know mom, I just can't do that yet. But I will be able to someday." I smiled and thought to myself: she knows.

I'm not saying that you will find greater meaning in your life by tending to dead animals on the side of the road: that is my personal path, and it may very well not be yours. The key is that if you choose to live an intentional life of awareness, these events become simple choices you make in your daily life.

Through one simple choice, I reaffirmed my commitment to following my own personal path, renewed my connection to creation and its cycles of life and death. An unexpected gift appeared, a resurgence of energy and an opportunity for deepening intimacy with my teenage daughter.

How do we learn how to live an intentional life in our everyday activities? The process is composed of three simple practices: *intention, awareness*, and *choice*.

It is essential to know the intention of your life. Who are you? What is the purpose of your life? Do you want to serve? Do you want to teach? Do you love to be near water? Do you want to work with animals? Do you enjoy working alone, or with others? What brings you passion and life? What makes your heart and mind soar? What are the intentions of your life? Your intentions lead you to your goals, your dreams, and your aspirations. Your life has infinite possibilities.

When we choose to live an intentional life, the first key is to develop the practice of awareness. We learn to listen to our lives and pay attention to what is important and what isn't.

We begin by practicing awareness. We become aware of where we are, what we are thinking, what we are doing. Many of us don't practice awareness because the more aware we become, the more engaged we are with the world around us. Though it is challenging, awareness is available to each of us. There is no longer room for pretending we can't hear, see, or smell the world around us.

When you practice awareness, the second part of the process is *choice*. As you develop your awareness, you bring a new light to everything you do. You see and experience things differently. You realize that you don't have to live in a pattern of habituation. You no longer feel like a victim with few choices in your life. You realize that everything in your life is truly the product of your choices. In every single thing you do, you are choosing a direction. Your life is a product of your choices. Through your choices, you become the hero of your life, not the victim.

Why should we change the way we are living in the world? Why would I clean a public bathroom? Why would I pick a dead dog up out of the road? Why should we bother to choose to live an intentional life? Is it worth the effort?

I promise you this: in the accumulation of seconds that create these moments of awareness, your intentional response can create a lifetime of joy. Your response to the everyday activities of your life can create immeasurable peace of mind, happiness and fulfillment. It is precisely these small things that create the avenues to the most fundamental changes within us. God—as they say—is in the details.

Why is this so hard for us to grasp? Perhaps because we live in a world where bigger, faster, and first are best. I choose the philosophy that suggests the smallest and the simplest things hold the greatest potential for transformation. The intentional life is uncovered in the smallest and the simplest of things in our lives. The most meaningful moments of our lives are already there, waiting to be discovered.

A Mother

I remember watching Mother Teresa being interviewed by a CNN correspondent once. He was awestruck that Mother Teresa had to date picked up some 30,000 sick and dying off the streets of Calcutta. This correspondent reverently looked into Mother Teresa's eyes and asked her, "How can you not get overwhelmed when you deal with so many sick and dying bodies? You have cared for thousands upon thousands of dying people personally. How can you continually do this?"

Mother Teresa was silent for a moment and then said, "The answer is simple, my son. I am with one soul at a time. I am fully present with the person I am with. As I look into each person's face, I see the face of Christ. I never think about yesterday, an hour from now, or tomorrow when I look into a person's eyes. It is never 30,000 people; it is one person at a time."

Her answer changed my life. We can become overwhelmed trying to do good in the world. We can become overwhelmed by choosing to give ourselves to too many causes, too many people; our lives feel flooded. Heed the words of Mother Teresa, and focus on one person at a time, one task at a time.

A Student

As a student chaplain at St. Joseph's Hospital many years ago, I dealt with a number of critical care patients. It is an intense experience to immerse oneself in the spiritual and physical needs of these individuals. I had become particularly attached to one elderly woman who was terminally ill. With no family and no hope of recovery, she lay in her room alone and despondent. Each day I went in and rubbed lotion into her beautiful old cracked and gnarled feet, read to her from her book of Psalms and sat in silence by her bed reverently listening to her shallow breathing. Her spirit seemed to grow as her body was dying. I found myself looking forward to our daily time together.

On a particularly overwhelming day, as the chaplain on call, I arrived at the hospital only to find my dear friend had died of a heart attack just that morning. As I stood before her lifeless frame, and my tears were welling in my eyes, my beeper went off. A beautiful sixteen-year-old girl had been in a tragic car accident during the night, and the doctors had declared her dead. As a chaplain, it was my responsibility to be present as we got permission to harvest organs for transplant. It was gut wrenching. As I sat with the parents and looked into the young girl's eyes, I couldn't believe the horrible pain in that room. I could hardly stand up, but I had to be strong for this family.

Barely an hour later, I found myself sitting with another set of grieving parents as we unplugged the respirator that kept their son alive. He had attempted suicide and was kept on the respirator until the doctors told them there was no hope.

As I was pulled from one tragic scene to another, I felt completely overwhelmed, unable to ease anyone else's pain. My teenage children at home suddenly seemed incredibly fragile and precious to me. I was confused about my faith, my work, my life—about everything. I started to walk back to the chaplain's on-call room, but instead I kept on walking, straight into the darkened chapel, where I collapsed onto the pew in tears.

After a few minutes, I began to sense a stillness growing within me. I remembered the plaque hanging over the desk in my office, a plaque given to me by a friend who was a chaplain as well. It read: "We can do no great things, only small things with great love." That quote is from Mother Teresa. I whispered it to myself over and over again in that hospital chapel that day. It helped me on that day and has become a part of my living an intentional life each day. It is a gentle reminder from a true authority on living an intentional life, Mother Teresa. In a world where bigger, more and faster is prized, it is a very valuable nugget of truth.

Everyday events, sometimes the most unlikely ones, are avenues to soulful experiences and the path to discover how to live an intentional life. Every day is filled with an abundance of such opportunities; every second is filled with a possibility of change. Did you take a shower today? Eat breakfast? Drive to work? It's time for you to discover how routine daily activities—not extraordinary events—hold the potential for you to live an intentional life.

CHAPTER ONE

Waking Up

ᕀ ᕀ ᕀ ᕀ ᕀ ᕀ ᕀ ᕀ ᕀ ᕀ

When you arise in the morning, give thanks for the morning light, for your life and strength. Give thanks for your food, and the joy of living. If you see no reason for giving thanks, the fault lies with yourself.

~Tecumseh, Shawnee Chief

ᕀ ᕀ ᕀ ᕀ ᕀ ᕀ ᕀ

DOES THIS SOUND LIKE YOU? The clock radio jerks you awake with Mick Jagger singing: "I can't get no satisfaction . . ." You reach over and slap the alarm button, then wearily swing your feet to the floor. Your partner grumbles unintelligibly. The cat loudly complains that breakfast is long overdue. And you're not sure what day it is.

Don't be Alarmed

More heart attacks occur in the morning than any other time—an "alarming" statistic for all of us who start each day leaping out of bed to meet the often overwhelming demands of family, career, and community. Consider how the average American wakes up: loud music or shrill radio voices startle and shock the body awake, the heart races, muscles contract, and adrenaline floods the system.

Instead, begin your day on a gentle note by replacing your clock radio with one of the many new alarms available that wake you to the soothing sounds of nature: rain, waves, wind, or a bubbling creek. You may want to wake up to your favorite CD of music or maybe someone's voice. Another great way to wake up gently is with an artificial sunrise alarm or lamp. Or plug your CD player or a bright light into an inexpensive timer to make a "clockless" alarm.

The sleep state is similar to being in our mother's womb: dark, peaceful, warm, connected. Emerging from sleep, therefore, can be seen as the birth process. If you think about waking up as just another routine matter, it becomes stale, old, common, and mundane. When you experience awakening each day as a metaphor for rebirth, you begin to live a life with new hope, promise and purpose.

Revitalize your Mornings

Before jumping out of bed, take three long slow deep abdominal breaths and bathe your sleepy organs in nourishing oxygen. Inhale. Exhale. Breath is the source of nourishment for your vital organs: brain, heart, and liver. It may seem simple, but breath is the easiest, most available conduit to emotional, physical, and spiritual well being.

In most languages, there is only one word meaning "breath" and "spirit": In Hindu, breath and spirit are called *prana*; in

Hebrew, *ruah*; and in Latin, *pneuma*. In English, however, "breath" and "spirit" are two separate words. When you restore the true meaning of "breath" on every level—physical, spiritual, and emotional—you develop a reverent respect for the simple process of breathing.

Take a few minutes to check in with yourself and scan your body head to toe. How do you feel? Do you have any pains? A headache? A giggly feeling in your stomach? Practice acknowledging and giving thanks for each organ, your arms, legs, skin, hair, and teeth.

There is intelligence in every cell of the body. When you scan your body, you are telling each of your cells that you are grateful for their daily functioning. According to the latest medical studies, communicating positively with your body causes measurable chemical and hormonal changes that boost the immune system and stimulate a healing response.

Imagine light, energy, a color, your favorite music, or water moving down your body. Thank your brain, spinal column, and brainstem for orchestrating the function of your body. Tell your eyes "thank you" for all the beauty you have seen. Tell your ears "thank you" for all the times you have heard "I love you." Continue this process, acknowledging and showing gratitude for every organ and system of your body.

Send loving thoughts to the places you will go and the people you will meet. Make a commitment to begin each day in peace and gratitude, and watch your life unfold with grace, ease, and serenity.

Intention, awareness, and choice can be applied to all your daily activities right from the moment you awake. How can you live a more intentional life? Simply begin with how you wake up in the morning.

Awakening Moments

Most great spiritual traditions contain moments of awakening. We find them with Mohammad in Islam, Saint Benedict in Christianity, Mary Baker Eddy in Christian Science, John Wesley in Methodism, and of course, the Buddha. In her book *Passages*, author Gail Sheehy observed that "If every day is an awakening, you will never grow old. You will just keep growing."

One of the great stories of all time about awakening is in the Buddhist tradition. In the last moments of the Buddha's life, his disciples surrounded him. They began to ask him, "Master, what last words of wisdom would you leave with us? After the many years of teachings and discourse, what is the most important final message you can leave with your devout followers?"

At the final moment of his life, Buddha opened his eyes, took his last breath, smiled, and said, "Wake up."

⚹ ⚹ ⚹ ⚹ ⚹ ⚹ ⚹ ⚹ ⚹

ALTER Your Waking Up

⚹ ⚹ ⚹ ⚹ ⚹ ⚹ ⚹

ASK YOURSELF:

How can I bring more peace to my morning routine?

Do I choose gratitude or grumpiness
first thing in the morning?

Can I take a few moments to sit quietly
and set my intention for my day?

TELL YOURSELF:

"I am grateful for each day."

GIVE YOURSELF:

- three long slow deep breaths first thing in the morning

- a quick self-massage of your face and scalp to get your blood circulating

- a framed quotation on your bedside table to remind you to begin each day with gratitude and reverence

CHAPTER TWO

The Shower

☀ ☀ ☀ ☀ ☀ ☀ ☀ ☀ ☀ ☀

If there is magic on this planet, it is contained in water.

~Loren Eiseley

☀ ☀ ☀ ☀ ☀ ☀ ☀

WATER BY ITS NATURE is invitational. It mesmerizes us. Water invites possibility and sends us deeper into ourselves. There is a sensual, sexual freedom associated with water. A simple shift in perspective on our daily shower can bring an invigorating sense of adventure, and become a source of power and connection with nature and ourselves.

There is no mystery why water is so significant to us. We are mostly water, about 75%. Brain tissue is 85% water, blood is 94% water, and even teeth are 5% water. Water is alive, filled with oxygen, minerals, and micronutrients.

Sacred Waters

The power of water is the power of invigoration and rebirth. Water rituals are used in purification, where they symbolize cleansing, refreshing, and new beginnings. We are formed in the moving water of our mother's womb. Our bodies and water are inextricably bound: when we enter the water, the body is literally coming home to itself.

Most traditions have rituals or ceremonies centered on water. The Cherokee perform a forgiveness ritual that involves going to the ocean or river and pouring water over oneself seven times to wash away guilt or bad memories. Muslims practice *wudu,* a ritual cleansing that prepares the mind, body, and spirit for prayer and meals. In Christianity, baptism is a sacramental ritual that initiates individuals into the body of the faithful.

The water of the Ganges and other sacred rivers in India are vital to prayer, blessing, healing, and dying rituals of the Hindu faith. Buddhism uses water in worship and considers rivers and lakes sacred and holy. Aboriginal peoples believe that the most holy water of all is moving and flowing: the water of rivers, waterfalls, and springs. Even the mythical Fountain of Youth promises eternal life.

These belief systems from around the world show us that there is power, potential and promise in the movement of water. With this in mind, you have the opportunity to experience your morning shower as a ritual of enchantment and renewal.

Power Shower

Water is the ultimate source of power. Imagine the power of a heavy summer rain massaging and cleansing your body, stimulating and invigorating your whole being, adding new life to your day. The movement of the water is critical in the morning because it transports you from the dormancy of sleep into the rhythms of the day. This simple shift in awareness can transform this seemingly mundane routine into an exciting and enriching daily ritual.

There is incredible energy in water. Moving water is powerful. Experience your shower as Niagara Falls. Absorb the energy and vibration of water, a frequency that energizes and invigorates. Your morning shower is your time. It is your morning rain, the beginning of the daily cycle of your life.

Imagine waterfalls, torrents of rain, raging rivers. Cultivating your imagination can be a portal to bliss in even the most ordinary circumstances. Remember the Herbal Essence shampoo commercial? An excited woman washes her hair as she luxuriates in the rush of a tropical waterfall. Her sensual moans sound orgasmic—and it's all in her imagination.

What a shower!

Singing in the Rain

Are you singing in your shower? Can you be as playful and joyous as Gene Kelly in the film *Singing in the Rain*? Water is irresistible—think children, sprinklers, and water guns. Why shouldn't your shower be playful? Try singing, chanting, or OM-ing in the shower. Imagine your shower as a new place every day of the week.

Practice mindfulness to set your intention for each shower. Is your intention to be invigorated? Soothed? Healed? You may need peace of mind. You may need freedom: freedom from pain, freedom from sorrow, guilt, possessions, relationships, or responsibility. Your intention may be to shed whatever is holding you in bondage. Allow the power of the water to wash away whatever you need to release, and imagine it flowing down the drain.

Challenge yourself with shower rituals and create your own. There can be annual rituals for holidays throughout the year. For example, on Thanksgiving, focus on being grateful for every part of your body, your health, your family, your home, your intelligence, your gifts and abilities. After each shower, briskly rub your arms, legs, and back with a towel to stimulate circulation, and tell every cell of your body that you are recommitting to an intentional life of gratitude. You can create rituals during different cycles of your life, at times of grieving, depression, illness, or joy.

The smallest changes you make in your daily shower can have astronomical effects. Historically there were few products offered for your shower. Zest deodorant soap promised to wake you up. Ivory promised purity. And Dove bar touted its beauty-cream richness. Today a whole new array of products are available for your shower. Be adventuresome: explore what scents, colors, and textures resonate with you.

Smell is the most powerful of our senses. Experiment with different scents according to your moods. On days that you feel lazy, tired or depressed, use an invigorating citrus flavor like lemon or orange. On mornings you wake up anxious, fearful, or nervous, you may want to choose the calming aromas of lavender, chamomile, or clary sage. You way want to choose a sensual scent such as jasmine or patchouli to feel amorous. Aromatherapy is not a passing fad: herbal and floral essences are shown to have an immediate effect on the brain and nervous system. There are many books on the market about aromatherapy to help you choose a scent for your particular need.

Experiment with the temperature of the water. A tepid or cooler shower can wake you up and invigorate you. A very hot shower can bring comfort and ease into your day. Recently shower hardware has become available that has automatic presets for the temperature. While this is a wonderful feature, don't let it lock you into a habit. Make sure you vary your shower temperature. You may want to start with a warm soothing shower, then end with a few seconds of brisk cool water to awaken and invigorate you.

Reclaim yourself in your morning shower and set the stage for the day. Your morning shower may be the only opportunity during the day when you have total freedom to make every single choice. Make the most of it.

❧ ❧ ❧ ❧ ❧ ❧ ❧ ❧ ❧ ❧

ALTER Your Shower

❧ ❧ ❧ ❧ ❧ ❧ ❧

ASK YOURSELF:

Is my shower area inspiring and happy?

How can I use my morning shower to
revitalize mind, body, and spirit?

Can I approach my shower with a childlike wonder
and appreciation for the gift of water?

TELL YOURSELF:

"Water refreshes and renews me."

GIVE YOURSELF:

• the opportunity to release negative emotions
and events

• soaps and shampoos in your favorite scents

• at least three times a day to reconnect with
water

CHAPTER THREE

Looking in the Mirror

ᴊᵏ ᴊᵏ ᴊᵏ ᴊᵏ ᴊᵏ ᴊᵏ ᴊᵏ ᴊᵏ ᴊᵏ ᴊᵏ

Our bodies communicate to us clearly and specifically,
if we are willing to listen to them.

~Shakti Gawain

ᴊᵏ ᴊᵏ ᴊᵏ ᴊᵏ ᴊᵏ ᴊᵏ ᴊᵏ

WHAT **DO YOU SEE** when you stand naked in front of your bathroom mirror? There are various answers to this question because we all have such diverse experiences of our bodies. We are each gloriously different, reflecting the infinite variety of humankind. We share the same anatomy, but different latitudes and longitudes. It is time for us to reframe the way we look at our own and each other's bodies.

Our current culture is awash in mixed messages about the body. While our Puritan heritage views the naked body as shameful or deviant, popular magazines, advertisements, television and movies bombard us with gratuitous nudity and hypersexuality. We live in a Barbie-doll culture where expectations are confusing and ambivalent. Unrealistic body images result in an epidemic of eating disorders and sexual confusion. Pacific island teens had virtually no incidence of anorexia or bulimia until the recent arrival of Western culture, when reports of these disorders suddenly soared.

As a result of this cultural onslaught, many of us live in a constant state of anxiety and obsession with the next great diet, miracle drug, exercise machine, or diet guru. It is time to disconnect from the automatic judgments and unreasonable expectations we saddle ourselves and each other with. It is time to turn a deaf ear to popular culture, to look at each other with our hearts, not our egos.

Did any of us really grow up wondering what size our mothers or grandmothers were? What mattered was the pure experience of the relationship. As a child, did you even notice size?

Begin by loving and accepting yourself, and you will naturally begin to view others with the same reverence. Look into the mirror at your body as it is *now*. Don't dwell on what you looked like in the past: when you were in school; before you were married; or how you might look in the future if you lost ten or fifteen pounds. Focus instead on how wonderful and miraculous your body is at this present moment.

Our Disembodiment

Western religions teach from the book of Genesis that we are *Imago Dei*—created in the image of God. If this is the promise of God, why is it so difficult for many of us to look at ourselves in the mirror? What have we been taught that brings pain, fear, anxiety, panic when we see the image of our own beautiful naked body? Only in industrialized nations do we bring such strong negative emotions to our own reflections.

Accepting our naked bodies may be one of our greatest personal journeys. Unfortunately, Western cultures have divided the body and soul: a division not made by Eastern cultures. Walt Whitman reminds us that "the body *is* the soul." Your soul experiences life through your body: the container, the vessel, and the organism by which it functions. Don't you think it's time to reconnect your body and soul?

Seeing Who is in the Mirror

Strive to accept your body and your form. There is a purpose and a reason for you to have the body you were born with. Our bodies are the stories of our lives. Each scar, wrinkle, and stretch mark records the events, journeys and stories of our lives.

Our bodies are majestic recording devices. Be mindful of your remarkable lifelong journey with your body, a journey which unfolds over time.

Let your body be your guide. Regular observation of your body is one of the best ways to maintain your health. Celebrate and embrace the natural changes, and tell your doctor about anything unusual. Seventy percent of all breast cancers are found through breast self-exams, not high-tech equipment. Keeping an eye on your body can literally save your life.

You may enjoy anointing your body daily with oil or cream. For many this may be uncomfortable to begin with, but over time you will look forward to reconnecting with your body every day. Choose a scent to match your mood.

Different aromas have distinct emotional and physiological effects. Your skin is an astounding organ. Your skin regulates your temperature and protects your body from bacteria and germs. Start with cream or oil at the top of your body and move down. Do so with great love, reverence, and respect for the fragile, sacred instrument we must nurture, respect, and care for. It is your body, after all, that enables you to experience the wonder of life.

✤ ✤ ✤ ✤ ✤ ✤ ✤ ✤ ✤

ALTER Your Mirror Image

✤ ✤ ✤ ✤ ✤ ✤ ✤

ASK YOURSELF:

When I see my image in the mirror, what emotions,
thoughts, and feelings do I experience?

Am I ready to give up criticism of my body?

Can I commit to appreciating and expressing gratitude
for my unique body when I look into the mirror?

TELL YOURSELF:

"I am perfect, whole, and complete just as I am."

GIVE YOURSELF:

- a new scented cream to put on your body each
  morning

- a moment in front of the mirror each day and
  say, "Thank You"

- a note on the mirror to remind you of your
  intentions for the day

CHAPTER FOUR

Breakfast

⚹ ⚹ ⚹ ⚹ ⚹ ⚹ ⚹ ⚹ ⚹ ⚹

All happiness depends on a leisurely breakfast.

~John Gunther

⚹ ⚹ ⚹ ⚹ ⚹ ⚹ ⚹

B REAKFAST IS THE MOST ABUSED, disrespected, irreverent meal of the day. We skip it, rush it or forget it. If we eat breakfast at all, most of us do so while running out the door, racing for the bus, or driving the car.

Just because breakfast has the word "fast" in it doesn't mean it should be a race. But sadly, a common breakfast scenario for many of us is a toaster pastry jammed in a pocket, coffee in one hand, briefcase and car keys in the other, as we fly out the door.

The standard American breakfast is often a junk-food fest: cereal bars, instant drinks, microwaveable packets of food. Many of us get our breakfast from fast-food drive-throughs or vending machines at work. Some of these foods can be nutritious, but too many of them are filled with excessive fat, sugar, and a tremendous number of calories. Complicating this is that most of this food is eaten standing, on the run, or in the car—hardly a mindful and relaxing mealtime.

The worst offense is skipping breakfast. If you eat supper at 7:00 p.m., then skip breakfast the next morning, you are literally fasting for 15 hours. Your body doesn't have what it needs to function, and your metabolism is slowed down for the entire day.

Breaking Fast

The word "breakfast" is derived from the phrase "breaking the fast." We fast while we sleep, and breaking that fast should make breakfast the most joyful meal of the day, as we have lived through the night and are beginning a new day. Breakfast is an opportunity for a new beginning that sets the stage—sets the table—for the day.

Do you remember the breakfasts at your grandmother's as a child? The smells and sounds that awakened you? The expectation of what you might find when you walked into the kitchen?

You knew that it would be something warm, nutritious, and above all, yummy. But there was much more to those breakfasts than simple calories and nutrition. You knew that you were being comforted, honored, and loved.

Breakfast is the first chance for loved ones to gather each day. As difficult as it may seem, sitting down together and sharing a meal can deepen intimacy over time and set a positive tone for the whole day. Even if it is only five minutes, that's five minutes together. Commit to five minutes each morning, and see any time over that as grace.

Slow down. Way way down. The faster you eat, the less aware you are of what you are putting into your body, and the more you shovel food in mindlessly. The more mindfully and slowly you eat, and the longer you chew, the greater the production of enzymes that ensure digestive health and facilitate the uptake of vital nutrients.

Be mindful of your morning meal. Make breakfast a banquet for all the senses by serving warm aromatic food on colorful dishes. Add flowers, playful napkins, a small book of your favorite sayings to contemplate. Pause before you start eating and look at your food. Be thankful for your food, your day, your time with those you love.

Consider the dozens of people who contributed to your meal: the farmers who grew it, the merchants who transported, stored, and sold it, the people who prepared it. Practice gratitude and respect for the nourishment on your plate and the process that brought it there. Pause and take a moment of silence before you pick up the fork.

Think you're too busy for breakfast? Then you are sacrificing much more than a simple meal. According to a study in *The Journal of the American College of Nutrition*, people who eat breakfast consume less fat and more carbohydrates. They have a higher intake of essential vitamins and minerals and lower serum cholesterol, which leads to a lower instance of heart disease.

Researchers from the Georgia Centenarian Study recently reported that people who reach the age of 100 tend to consume breakfast more regularly than those who skip the first meal of the day. And dozens of studies show that people who eat plenty of fruits and vegetables generally have a lower risk of heart disease, cancer, and other chronic diseases.

Sadly, the incidence of Type 2 diabetes among children is rising at an alarming rate, in large part due to sugary breakfasts and snacks. A healthy balanced breakfast of protein, carbohydrate, and fruit can be a vital disease prevention tool for children and set lifelong patterns of good nutrition.

Medical studies reveal that people who eat breakfast regularly show increases in learning ability, attention span, and a general well being. Conversely, people who skip breakfast show an increase in weight gain and memory impairment.

Eating breakfast increases your metabolic rate by 25 percent, which is one of the reasons why people report feeling better early in the morning. The American Heart Association suggests that you may be more prone to diabetes and obesity if you skip your morning meal because breakfast helps control your appetite for the rest of the day.

Break Feast

You don't have to wake up in time to cook a huge breakfast. It only takes 5–10 minutes to eat a bowl of cereal with low-fat milk and fruit. Try yogurt mixed with your cereal. If you don't like traditional breakfast food, eat a sandwich. Eat frozen waffles or pancakes with fruit or light syrup. This is a great time to be creative with what's in the refrigerator. Mix leftover vegetables from last night's dinner with scrambled eggs. What matters is that you are eating *something* and that it is relatively healthy: preferably with protein, fruit, and fiber.

By eating breakfast, you honor your body, your family, and your day.

ALTER Your Breakfast

ASK YOURSELF:

What are five quick and nutritious breakfasts I can have on hand?

How can I make breakfast more relaxed for myself and my loved ones?

Can we, as a family, commit to sit together for 5 minutes at breakfast?

TELL YOURSELF:

"Breakfast is the feast that celebrates the beginning of my day."

GIVE YOURSELF:

- a special bowl or mug to remind you to start your day mindfully
- festive breakfasts to mark celebrations and holidays
- the luxury of a long leisurely breakfast on the weekends

CHAPTER FIVE

The Morning News

❦ ❦ ❦ ❦ ❦ ❦ ❦ ❦ ❦ ❦

Men are disturbed not by things that happen,
but by their opinion of the things that happen.

~Epictetus

❦ ❦ ❦ ❦ ❦ ❦ ❦

O N TELEVISION TODAY, there are regular morning shows on almost every network that bring you the day's soft news. These are filled with human-interest stories; what's new in the home; tidbits on relationships; cultural profiles; celebrity sightings; and breaking developments concerning your health and happiness. These morning shows have become a form of social conditioning that subtly tells you what is expected of you, what you should wear, what you should look like, what you should drive, what you should fear. They set a personal agenda that may or may not be in tune with your authentic self.

Infotainment

Television's "good morning" shows feature "infotainment": a rather confusing jumble of information and entertainment that our American culture has become addicted to. Our daily lives are interwoven with sound bites and video clips. We expect weather every fifteen minutes, traffic on the half-hour, and the latest celebrity dish in between. For many of us, we expect every aspect of our lives to be entertaining.

But we have a choice—we can filter what we take into our ears, eyes, minds, and lives. By practicing mindfulness we can battle the overload of information and sort out what serves and supports our authentic selves.

Continuing Education

Choose what you want to actively learn in the morning. What aspects of our popular culture do you really need to be in touch with? Instead of the morning news being background noise, intentionally screen for information that matters to you: select the information that will enhance and benefit your life.

Look to the morning as a time to get information about what is going on in the world—not news-wise—but rather, exercise your curiosity about books, medical studies, politics or the latest trends. Choose information that enriches your intentional life. Actively structure your watching or listening towards items you are interested in. Try alternative media sources like NPR or the BBC for different perspectives. Use the morning news as a class-room. Take the snippets of information you are receiving, find something that interests you, then use that as a starting point on a journey to research other sources of information: the library, the internet, bookstores, a class or seminar.

⚓ ⚓ ⚓ ⚓ ⚓ ⚓ ⚓ ⚓ ⚓

ALTER Your Morning News

⚓ ⚓ ⚓ ⚓ ⚓ ⚓ ⚓

ASK YOURSELF:

Do my current television habits restore and
refresh me, or do they deplete me?

What are my areas of interest on the morning news?

How can listening to the
morning news educate me?

TELL YOURSELF:

"New information helps me grow and
learn more about this world."

GIVE YOURSELF:

- variety in your choice of morning shows

- a moment to send good thoughts to anyone in
  the news who needs it

- a notebook to jot down items you may want to
  learn more about

CHAPTER SIX

Commuting

✻ ✻ ✻ ✻ ✻ ✻ ✻ ✻ ✻ ✻

*"If you do what you've always done,
you'll get what you've always gotten."*

~Anonymous

✻ ✻ ✻ ✻ ✻ ✻ ✻ ✻

EVERY DAY MILLIONS OF US SPEND HOURS in our automobiles. Thirty-four percent of Americans spend 30 minutes or more on their daily commute—that's over 250 hours per year! Five days a week, morning and evening, we race for the best seat on the train, the last spot on the bus, the fastest lane on the highway, the choicest parking space in the lot. Increasingly, we can feel angry and frustrated at others for being in our way; at worst, we can feel victimized, out of control, insignificant.

These psychological dynamics can lead to higher blood pressure, higher levels of stress hormones, and serious consequences for our family, our relationships, and our work. Road rage is on the rise, and research suggests that the more stress drivers feel during their morning commute, the more problems they have in the workplace.

Commuting has become a time of isolation, aggression and alienation. Several recently released studies suggest that the more hassled drivers feel by their morning commute, the more verbally abusive they are to co-workers. These drivers can also attempt to sabotage productive efforts at work. We can't rely upon Detroit or Tokyo to provide a solution, because the auto industry has given us videos, phones and GPS systems, gadgets that seem to lead us further and further away from our true selves into an even more distracted and frenetic state.

It's time to gain a new perspective on our commute. Maybe you can't change your commute, but you can change your actions and attitudes, and transform your daily drive from a strain on your nerves to a nurturing, replenishing journey that leaves you ready to face your day or evening.

Transformational Space

Commuting is packed with options for health and renewal. Your commute can become your own personal classroom, temple, behavioral laboratory, concert hall or choir loft, depending on your needs. For many, commuting is a rare time to be alone. Choose to learn something new in this precious time. Feed your mind with books on tape. Take along a quotation or prayer to memorize, or use mindfulness beads to bring you back to awareness. Breathe deeply as you tense and release each muscle in your body. Keep a list of affirmations to repeat during traffic jams.

Or turn your car into a counseling center or behavioral laboratory. Focus on one specific attitude or behavior you wish to change. Pick an attitude or behavior such as anger or pessimism, smoking or overeating, and focus on it for a week. Find and listen to tapes on that attitude or behavior you are interested in learning about. You can find tapes and CDs at bookstores, online, or at the malls. If you see a counselor, discuss your morning commute; he or she can be a great resource of innovative ideas and materials. Renew your commitment to disconnect your "autopilot" and live an intentional life. Utilize your 250 hours per year to *evolve*, not *devolve*.

On your commute you may discover a concert hall. Your commute is a good time to listen to stress-reducing music. Be gentle to your ears, and choose what you listen to mindfully. Talk radio and top 40 radio, with their brash announcers and harsh advertisements, can over-stimulate you, increasing your anxiety level. Instead, explore the restorative power of music. Psychologists have long heralded the power of a person's favorite music to calm the emotions and relieve stress. Find what works for you and give yourself the gift of music that truly nourishes your mind, body and soul. Whether you are on a bus, train, car or airport, you can calm yourself by listening to beautiful music on a CD or tape player with earphones.

Your commute may be an experience in your own choir loft. Or take a cue from the birds and sing your way to work. Singing releases physical tension, oxygenates the blood, and expresses suppressed emotion, revitalizing and renewing mind, body and spirit. By stimulating the right brain, singing can increase your creative and problem-solving abilities at work. Your co-workers will wonder what's come over you when you bounce into work radiant and energetic.

Your commute can become a classroom. Have you ever wanted to learn a foreign language, increase you vocabulary, or study philosophy? You may not have time at home or work, but you can use your commuting time to learn. Almost every book published these days is available in audio. You can listen to a new book each week and learn more than you ever dreamed. You can change your life dramatically just by turning your car into a classroom.

Could your car, train, bus or airplane be your temple? You don't have to experience this time as wasted, lost or not meaningful. Always travel with an inspirational book, meditation or prayer beads, journal or a shawl. When you get stuck in traffic, whether on a plane, train or in an automobile, you can choose to connect with your Source.

People have been using beads for praying and meditating since the beginning of humankind. Beads have a calming affect on us and help us focus. You can wrap yourself in a comfortable shawl, take some deep breaths, and pray or meditate as you slowly count off your beads. Meditate on a mantra or on inspiring words to comfort you and teach you how to live an intentional life.

We're All in This Together

To counteract the alienating effect of being isolated in your car in what seems like a mad dash to nowhere, consider that no time is wasted, lost, or meaningless. The commute is an excellent time to experience yourself as part of the human family. Look around you at the infinite variety of human beings. Honor each person you see: consider that, at their core, they share the same fears and dreams as you.

We are not in a competition with other cars, and our fellow commuters are not the enemy. We all share the highway. We are all on merging paths. Despite what our bumper stickers may proclaim, we have far more in common than we think. We can give and take and share on our commute, deepening and strengthening our inner experience that we are not separate, competing for the same resources, but together, sharing in the abundant flow of creation. Even alone in our cars, we can feel connected to others.

Practice fundamental virtues on your commute—surrender to the process, and, before you know it, positive thoughts and emotions will become a naturally restorative part of your daily life. Practice patience and generosity by allowing someone to merge in front of you. When a driver unintentionally cuts you off, practice compassion by smiling at his or her preoccupation. If it seems as though the world around you is losing its mind, practice courage by refusing to participate in the group mindset. When it begins to storm, practice intention by asking that all the drivers on the road arrive home safely.

Above all, practice being peaceful and centered on your commute—it's the ultimate way to strengthen your inner ability to remain calm. It's easy to feel at peace during a meditation or yoga class, or sitting beside a remote mountain lake at sunset, but your real opportunity to exercise your inner calm comes in chaotic circumstances—and there's no better place than a traffic jam to actively practice serenity, compassion, and gratitude: three practices at the foundation of a balanced and fulfilling life.

As you commute, you control more than just the brake and steering wheel: you also have the power of choice over your attitudes, thoughts, and emotions. You can choose to create anger, frustration, alienation, and anxiety, or you can choose to use this time alone for self-reflection, mindfulness, personal growth and renewal. Exercise your power to *choose.*

ꙮ ꙮ ꙮ ꙮ ꙮ ꙮ ꙮ ꙮ ꙮ ꙮ

ALTER Your Commute

ꙮ ꙮ ꙮ ꙮ ꙮ ꙮ ꙮ

ASK YOURSELF:

Do I hold my breath, clench my teeth,
or tighten my muscles when I drive?

What can I do to remind myself to be more
mindful during my commute?

How can I refresh and renew myself
during my commute?

TELL YOURSELF:

"I choose serenity in busy places."

GIVE YOURSELF:

- three deep breaths at each stoplight
- your favorite author on audiotape or CD
- the joy of singing your heart out

CHOICE

The Power of Choice

The Cabin

AS I PUSHED OPEN THE OLD LOG CABIN DOOR, two black scorpions rushed across the planked floors and disappeared into the fireplace. An unfriendly welcome, but I knew there was no turning back. A faint light filtered through closed shutters. It smelled musty and moldy; I was sure the room hadn't been opened in years. The old wood floor creaked as I slowly walked across it to open the shutters and invite the daylight in.

Standing in the midst of dancing cobwebs and swirling dust, I realized I had taken my first step on a journey with no map, no directions and no clear destination. In the stark silence of that moment, a certain sense of peace swept across the room and engulfed me. I knew my choice to live an intentional life would change the rest of my life, and, for the first time, I sensed the adventure and the uncertainty of my choice.

The cabin had no electricity, no water, no gas, no kitchen, and no bathroom. I surveyed the outside and discovered the outhouse and a rain barrel on the far side of the cabin. Back on the front porch, I snuggled into an old rocker that had been left behind. And in anticipation of the days ahead, I pulled a scrap of paper from my pocket to write on.

As I began making a list of "how-to" books I would need on plumbing, construction, and electrical work, a rush of energy and a sense of power surged deeply through my body. I grinned as I rocked back and forth in the tattered rocker that creaked with each rock. In this primitive cabin in the north Georgia mountains, I was a long way from my previous life.

The Unintentional Life

I was working in New York City, flying back and forth to Atlanta each week. My life was a hectic race. But I had all the trappings of success measured by our culture. As a stockbroker at a Wall Street firm, I was set on a model of doing everything faster and better than any of my competitors.

My aspiration was to have it all. I am the oldest daughter in a family of seven children and groomed for self-reliance. From the time I was a little girl, I wanted to be a successful woman. For me, that meant having an upwardly mobile career, a successful husband, perfect children, a nice home, a great car, elegant clothes, and fabulous vacations. I constantly worked to keep a perfect dress size and drove the ultimate driving machine to match.

My life was very well calculated and moving at a planned, orchestrated pace, when one day—in a split second—everything stopped.

I had landed at the airport as usual early Monday morning and grabbed a cab to the World Trade Center. I got out of the cab, entered the building, and headed for the elevator. All of a sudden, my chest was so tight I could hardly breathe. We were all packed into the elevator as usual, but this time as it sped up to my office, I thought I was having a heart attack. I lurched off the elevator and lay against the wall.

Three hours later, I was still against the same wall and hadn't moved an inch. An attentive security guard had noticed—and perhaps because he had seen it before—made a diagnosis of a panic attack.

Little did I know that would be first of many to follow. It wasn't too long until insomnia began to haunt me at night, while panic attacks continued to plague me during the day. I became obsessively aware of the people that surrounded me each day.

Along with the panic attacks and insomnia, a new keen sense of awareness began to emerge. As I went to work each day, I noticed we all seemed to look and act like zombies. It felt like we were trained to do the same thing over and over again. I noticed how people were buying lunch from a sidewalk cart then mindlessly eating as they walked away. Everywhere I looked, everyone and everything began to look the same. It seemed as if we were all in some trance. My well-designed life had started to unravel.

Later, still in New York, I was studying for my commodity boards when I stumbled upon an old copy of Thoreau's journal in the apartment where I was staying. I dusted off the front of the book, turned to the first page and it read:

I went to the woods because I wished to live deliberately, to front only the essential facts of life, and see if I could not learn what it had to teach, and not, when I came to die, discover that I had not lived.

Little did I know his words would change my life forever.

My initial response to that famous passage was shock, confusion, and an indescribably immense sadness. Was I living deliberately? Was I living an intentional life? How in the heck did I know what the essential facts of life were? And if I die tomorrow, have I really lived at all? Is living in the middle of this rat race really living?

Thoreau's words made me painfully aware that the course I had charted for my life was far from "intentional." I had carved out an outwardly "successful" life, and it had become a prison of my own design. My life had nothing to do with my authentic self or with an awareness of my own desires and dreams.

I had not been in the woods since I was a child. I knew nothing about the realities of living in nature, and the mere thought that nature held the possibility of teaching me something both intrigued and terrified me. A fundamental shift occurred in that moment, and I knew there was no turning back.

One week later, I purchased a farm with an old log cabin that sat by a lake. There wasn't even a road into the cabin from a main road. I had to hike to the cabin for the first year. I was determined to live up to Thoreau's challenge. I was going to face the challenge of living an intentional life. I would turn this land into a working farm. With each step, I chose to release the life I had so masterfully orchestrated and designed, and I surrendered to the unfolding of an intentional life.

My choice to surrender had begun.

Surrender

It wasn't until some years later that I would come to a stronger understanding of the enormous inner power that came from practicing surrender. In my fiercely competitive sports and business-driven family, "surrender" was a dirty word. "Surrender" meant loss, failure, being conquered; it evoked the image of a white flag with a defeated person marching across the battlefield. Surrender was—and still is—the most difficult practice to embrace.

Surrender is one of the most powerful choices you can make. When you choose to surrender, you release your ego and your attachment to life the way you have constructed it. When you surrender, you trust in and join a power much greater that your own. As you practice surrender, there is an uncanny synergy in every action of your life. Life becomes exciting, dynamic, and meaningful. You know that you are living an intentional life because you are fully present and completely yourself in every situation. You live in a state of confidence.

Surrender was the most difficult practice for me. It was counter-intuitive and terrifying to let go and trust the power of my choices. Many inspiring teachers taught me how to surrender and why surrender held the key to what was holding me back in my own life. I had learned at an early age how powerful the feeling of control is, or at least the illusion of control I experienced.

I learned that if I really wanted to live an intentional life, I had to surrender to the process that I was learning from age-old, time-honored traditions and mentors I admired in our world, who had discovered their own great purpose in life by surrendering.

A Great Teacher

After I left the brokerage firm and moved to the woods, I had the privilege to study with many great teachers who each demonstrated the power of choice and surrender on a daily basis. One of my great teachers was former U.S. President and Nobel Peace Prize winner Jimmy Carter. President Carter taught a class in ethics when I was in seminary at Emory University. He talked about his experience in the White House and the difficult choices he had to make, knowing full well that many of these choices would not make him popular and could cost him re-election. Yet he chose to surrender to his deep sense of truth rather than political expediency. He would not compromise his choice to live an intentional life.

After he lost his bid for re-election, President Carter was somewhat depressed and confused. He spent some time wrestling with his emotions, then made a conscious choice to surrender to the pain of his loss, to honor his inner voice, and devote his life to making the world a better place for others. He began with his unshakeable belief in the democratic process, and started traveling to dangerous third-world countries to monitor elections because he believed that every person, no matter what his or her position in life, had a right to the ballot box.

When his wife, Rosalynn and he traveled to Africa, they discovered that a tremendous number of people there were infected with the Guinea worm, a devastating parasite that is transmitted by drinking stagnant water. This worm can grow to be over three feet long in the human body, and can cause horrible pain and death.

The Carters were overwhelmed with compassion for the senseless suffering of the people afflicted with this disease. Together, they made a choice: they would work to eradicate this terrible condition through a grassroots movement of support and education. In the years they have dedicated their lives to this project, the ripple effect of that choice they made has successfully eradicated 99% of the disease. President Carter and Rosalynn are now pushing to complete the task and eliminate the remaining 1% of the disease in Africa.

Thanks to the Carters and the people who work side-by-side with them, Guinea worm disease, which was once a horrible plague, will soon be only a memory. They are a living example of the power of choice and surrender. They embrace a life open to each new circumstance on their path—no matter how small—as an opportunity to choose, surrender and continually be renewed.

The Stall

Not so long ago, I was sitting in the corner of the stall at my stables after foaling out a mare, and I reflected on the choices I have made in my own life. I now live in the woods full-time, and it has taught me much. Many lessons have come to me as I built this farm and made the choice to live an intentional life.

Many incredible people have inspired me along the way: the ninety-year-old farmer down the road that still makes hominy and cans his own sauerkraut; the eighty-eight-year-old, near-blind woman who made me a prize-winning quilt at the county fair; my elderly patient who has survived both legs being amputated, blindness and renal dialysis, but still responds to life with a smile on her face. There are so many simple, holy people in the woods who have taught me a lot. As I slowed down and listened to their stories, I discovered the profound depth of their awareness. These teachers of mine have created intentional lives of their own choosing. I am also blessed with the four-legged angels that inspire me daily: my dogs, cats, and horses.

Most people would see the surrender of a life on Wall Street to a life in a log cabin in the North Georgia woods as opposite ends of the scale. By comparison to what others have done, I realize every day my goal is to live an intentional life, and I still have very far to go.

It takes one courageous step at a time. People who live extraordinary lives are in fact ordinary people who make choices that lead to extraordinary circumstances. These choices are often very small, and these choices are available to you.

Our lives are filled with seemingly mundane, everyday tasks, tasks we often mindlessly or begrudgingly complete as quickly as we can. Perhaps because we live in a world where bigger, faster, and first are seen as best, often the smallest and simplest things are dismissed or overlooked. But it is these small, simple everyday moments that can be a gateway to growth and renewal. Routine activities such as working, shopping, and reading—not extraordinary events—hold the potential to bring you a life of greater peace, balance, and contentment.

CHAPTER SEVEN

Working

✳ ✳ ✳ ✳ ✳ ✳ ✳ ✳ ✳ ✳

"Work is love made visible. And if you cannot work with love but only with distaste, it is better that you should leave your work and sit at the gate of the temple and take alms of those who work with joy."
~Kahlil Gibran

✳ ✳ ✳ ✳ ✳ ✳ ✳

W HEN WE THINK OF WORK, the image that comes to mind for most in the Western world is one of intense productivity. As a result, the American workplace is often the most spiritually barren space many of us experience. The requirement to make business decisions based on bottom-line thinking often eliminates making decisions based on achieving work-life balance. Maintaining a balance in our work and life in the American workplace is an extraordinary challenge.

These days the paths of profit and work-life balance rarely cross. Fifty-five percent of American workers say their workday leaves them overtired and overwhelmed. And forty percent rate their jobs as stressful or extremely stressful. The recent economic shift, with its downsizing and layoffs, has only exacerbated the problem: workers left behind find themselves saddled with twice as much work for the same amount of pay.

A great number of employees in the industrial world are dissatisfied with their life at work. Our current culture tends to see work primarily as a means to make money—which translates into purchasing more. In our work-centric world, our job titles have become the primary expression of our identity. The first question most of us ask upon meeting is: "What do you do for a living?" Our other roles—as parent, child, friend; teacher, leader, mentor; poet, painter, dancer; craftsman, musician, athlete—are often diminished or devalued as being "non-productive," especially if they don't "bring home the bacon."

We often experience our jobs as nothing more than apathetic habituation—hollow, empty, and meaningless—a mundane task that earns a benefit package. Our current mindset has stripped work of its authentic purpose and consequently stripped us of the dignity of performing meaningful work.

For many of us, work has become an acceptable addiction: workaholism is the number one socially sanctioned way to escape one's self and one's family. We have 12-step programs and treatment centers for every addiction imaginable, but so far, no "Betty Ford" of workaholism has stepped forward to speak the sad truth.

Productivity protocols, time and motion studies, assembly lines, and cubicles all serve to accelerate our rhythms, isolate and alienate us. The business world's bottom-line thinking almost always precludes more global considerations such as worker happiness, family unity, environmental health, or social justice.

Maintaining balance and living an intentional life in the American earnings per share workplace is one of the greatest challenges of the 21st century. It may take courage and perseverance, but it is possible to reframe our experience in the workplace, and reclaim our labor as dignified, our laborers as noble.

Outer Work, Inner Work

What calls us out of this gloomy scenario is our *intention* to experience work as a calling, a vocation, an art, science, or craft; to see the workplace as a vital community; to understand work as just one important component of a healthy balance of activities that nurture mind, body, soul.

Freud said work is the basis of sanity, and spiritual leaders throughout time have shown us that work can be sacred. To the Benedictine monastic order, work is holy because it makes us "whole-ly." Work is not seen as punishment or penance, but as participation in creation. Work is honored as a powerful source of purpose, renewal, and dignity.

Instead of experiencing work as isolating and alienating, we can begin to see our work as meaningful and valuable. Instead of divorcing ourselves from our role as co-creators with the Divine, we can choose to experience work as an awe-inspiring example of the interconnectedness of all creation.

A friend who worked for a large greeting card company despaired about sitting hunched over in her cramped cubicle, drawing dancing bears and unicorns day after day, while her art school friends worked in their lofts and invited her to openings at the top galleries. She became more and more dissatisfied, barely able to haul herself out of bed in the morning, until one day a colleague pointed out that every product she created was used at birthdays, weddings, and other celebrations that brought people closer together. Her sometimes "corny" products were important tokens people used to connect to each other and express the deepest feelings of their hearts—feelings they often had no words for.

She stopped to consider the awesome power of even the most mundane get-well card to convey love, caring, and healing. This simple shift in perspective—seeing how deeply she was connected to her fellow beings, and honoring her true role in co-creation—brought a renewed vigor to her work and an added surge in creativity and satisfaction.

"Co-creation" means that each of us participates in the process of creation. Most of us at some point in our lives have had the experience of being a conduit for something greater than ourselves: as we build, teach, sell, or dance, our work is co-creation with others and with the Divine. We can literally become the hands, feet, and voice of our intention to make this world a better place.

Your work can bring both prosperity and fulfillment. When you surrender to the natural process of growth and service and choose to experience your work as life-giving and abundant, before you know it your outer work will begin to reflect your inner work.

Cubicles as Classrooms

Try reframing your workplace as an ongoing "intentional life" seminar, a school where you can learn and grow. Consider that everyone is at work to teach you something—it may be as simple as a new skill or business tip, or as profound as patience and understanding. Each person you encounter has the possibility to challenge and ultimately transform you.

Make conscious choices about how you approach and handle situations. You can learn a great deal about others from work and you can learn about yourself as well. Cultivate your ability to frame events in this larger, universal context: the ability to "see the big picture" is a cornerstone of work-life balance.

One of the most common business problems, for example, is dealing with anger that arises from office politics and perceived inequities. It can take courage and perseverance to stay true to your authentic self. Addressing uncomfortable situations in a mindful way may seem challenging, but ultimately it will bring more peace, deeper communication, and increased vitality and creativity to your workday.

If your job is a classroom, and you stop learning, find another classroom. Make work-life balance part of your intentional life so that when you do have to go through the inevitable transitions of the modern economy, you do not collapse because your "life is your work."

Cultivate curiosity and creativity at work—the great thinkers and leaders of our time all displayed a playful curiosity about life. Look for the greatest good in the smallest task. Practice gratitude for the ability to make a living, to work in a safe workplace, and to serve others.

Deepen your listening skills—close your mouth, quiet your mind and body, and truly listen to what your boss or colleague is saying. Listen not with a racing mind, but with a quiet heart. See if—just for a moment—you can experience what it is like to be in his or her shoes.

Practice being respectful of your co-workers. See their diversity as a unique opportunity to learn and experience the commonalities of all human beings. Examine your conversations, memos, and e-mails with your colleagues. Put each form of communication to the test of ancient Sufi wisdom: Is it true? Is it necessary? Is it fair?

Be mindful that conflict, when it arises, is an excellent opportunity for growth. Regardless of how it may seem, you don't have to react immediately. Pause to calm your mind and relax your body before you respond. Inhale. Exhale. Recall your deepest intentions. Then carefully consider your response.

Work is Play

A childlike ability to see possibilities for variety and creativity can transform even the most mundane workplace into a haven of life and renewal. Soften an institutional environment by bringing natural objects into your workspace: a plant, a bowl of fruit or a favorite stone. Post inspirational sayings and artwork. Smile for no reason. Pack your lunch in a Wonder Woman lunch box. Keep your inner child alive, for your inner child is a great source of happiness, energy, creativity, and connectedness.

When we explore and reframe who we are with respect to our work and our co-workers, we discover our true passion. We uncover who we were meant to be and what we were meant to do. And our work becomes one nurturing element—not the center—of a balanced, intentional life.

✤ ✤ ✤ ✤ ✤ ✤ ✤ ✤ ✤ ✤

ALTER Your Work

✤ ✤ ✤ ✤ ✤ ✤ ✤

ASK YOURSELF:

In what ways do I make the world a
better place through my work?

How is the purpose of my life
unfolding through my work?

What are my most challenging relationships
at work? How can I reframe them,
and what can I learn from them?

TELL YOURSELF:

"Everyone I meet is my teacher."

GIVE YOURSELF:

• quiet time during your workday to center
  yourself, focus and refresh

• lunch with a co-worker you don't know very
  well

• a "workspace makeover" with office accessories
  that reflect your commitments and passions

CHAPTER EIGHT

Walking

ᴕ ᴕ ᴕ ᴕ ᴕ ᴕ ᴕ ᴕ ᴕ ᴕ

"He who sits still in a house all the time
may be the greatest vagrant of all; but the saunterer,
in the good sense, is no more vagrant than
the meandering river, which is all the while
sedulously seeking the shortest course to the sea.
For every walk is a sort of crusade."

~Henry David Thoreau

ᴕ ᴕ ᴕ ᴕ ᴕ ᴕ ᴕ

NO ONE IS MORE REVERED for deepening our connection to the joy of walking than Henry David Thoreau. For Thoreau, walking was a spiritual practice, an opportunity to explore nature, and an avocation that led to him becoming one of the foremost conservationists of all time. Thoreau warned us that when we do not experience nature to its fullest, we may eventually erode our freedom and wildness, our lifeline to creation and the Creator.

Thoreau challenged us to experience walking as a crusade or an adventure with an intention. Challenge yourself to share Thoreau's passion for the humble stroll.

Step by Step

Saunter, saunter, saunter: it's a revered historical practice. As we saunter along, we walk the path of our lives. Buddha spent his life walking from village to village, sitting with his disciples in small groups beneath trees. Jesus walked from town to town to heal the sick and speaking to gatherings of people outdoors.

Mahatma Gandhi trod the 150 miles of his Salt March in reaction to the British occupation of India's salt mines. And he didn't stop walking after that. Rather, he lived on his feet, walking for social justice and transforming a nation.

Dr. Martin Luther King, Jr. walked the roads of Mississippi, Alabama, and Georgia, seeking to heal the hatred that divided our country. Susan B. Anthony spent her entire life walking so that women could participate in the democratic process through voting. Walking, as an empowering, community building force—is one of the cornerstones of social justice.

The Australian aborigines go on "walkabout" when they are in need of healing. Native Americans walk the earth as a daily sacred practice. Christian monastics, Islamic Sufis, Buddhist disciples, virtually all faiths make walking meditation part of a deeply grounded spirituality.

Pilgrimages are a part of almost every spiritual tradition and belief system. From historical times until today, Jews go to Jerusalem; Christians go to the Holy Land; Muslims go to Mecca. When we participate in a pilgrimage, we join a community of kindred spirits. Our journey together connects us, deepens us.

Rich and poor, ignorant and educated, all walk the same path toward the same destination.

Walking 101

The frenzy of moving treadmills, Stairmasters, sidewalks, escalators, elevators, and of course cars has disconnected us from an appreciation of walking. No one needs to be reminded of the power of walking to restore and improve physical health, but walking is far more than just a simple cardiovascular exercise.

Vietnamese Buddhist monk Thich Nhat Hanh, famous for teaching us "walking meditation," reminds us to hold the intention of being fully present in the moment each step on our life's path. As you walk, feel your foot come into contact with the earth. Experience the rhythm and flow of your stride as a symphony. Marvel in the harmony of your arms, legs, and trunk; release past burdens and future fears as you surrender to the present moment.

Get out of your car, get off your bike, get off the bus one stop early, and *walk*. Use this time to practice serenity, reflection, and awareness. Notice the wind, the changes of the seasons. Connect to the birds, the trees, the mystical alchemy of Nature. Look, smell, listen. Allow your senses to become keenly aware and profoundly energetic. In the dance of mindfulness and awareness, our senses are heightened as we empty ourselves into the now.

Challenge the curiosity of the explorer who lies within you. Take the less traveled road, change your route, choose a different path. And above all, follow the advice of Henry David Thoreau: "We should go forth on the shortest walk, perchance, in the spirit of undying adventure, never to return."

❧ ❧ ❧ ❧ ❧ ❧ ❧ ❧ ❧ ❧

ALTER Your Walk

❧ ❧ ❧ ❧ ❧ ❧ ❧

ASK YOURSELF:

"How can I add more walking to my day?"

"How can I bring variety to my walking routine?"

"How can I deepen and enrich my experience of walking?"

TELL YOURSELF:

"I feel power enter my body with each step."

GIVE YOURSELF:

- a long walk with a good friend

- a walking meditation

- new and different roads to walk

CHAPTER NINE

Exercising

⚹ ⚹ ⚹ ⚹ ⚹ ⚹ ⚹ ⚹ ⚹ ⚹

Do your thing and you will have the power.

~Ralph Waldo Emerson

⚹ ⚹ ⚹ ⚹ ⚹ ⚹ ⚹

IT IS CRITICAL—LITERALLY FOR THE LENGTH and quality of our lives—that we educate ourselves about the importance of exercise during our entire life. Consider how magnificently exercise benefits our health and well-being. Exercise lowers blood pressure, reduces cholesterol, and controls blood sugar. It strengthens and builds muscle tone and bones; increases energy levels; reduces body fat; and helps increase the strength of the heart. It prevents heart disease, cancer, arthritis, and a host of other serious medical conditions.

Exercise alleviates stress, anxiety, and depression. It strengthens the immune system, stimulating "natural killer cells" which play a vital role in fighting cancer, bacteria, and viruses.

Our bodies were meant to *move*: lack of activity contributes to a host of physical and psychological disorders. Robert M. Butler, MD of Mt. Sinai Medical School in New York proclaims, "If exercise could be packaged into a pill, it would be the single most prescribed and beneficial medication in the nation."

Exercise Your Imagination

So if it's so good for us, why do we dislike it so much? Exercise in America has often been experienced as penance, punishment and ordeal. We see exercise as competition, and our failure to "measure up" as defeat.

But if you choose to see yourself as vigorous and fit, instead of "not measuring up," in time your very cell structure will mirror the pictures you hold in your mind. Just as Eastern practices such as martial arts, yoga, tai chi, or chi gong are readily understood as mind/body disciplines, you can re-imagine your everyday routine and experience any form of exercise as a vehicle to refresh and renew mind, body, and soul. Practice awareness as you do jumping jacks, lift weights, or pound away on your elliptical machine. Repeat a mantra or affirmation with each movement. Keep your attention in your body and on your breathing, and you will restore yourself on multiple levels.

Exercise is an essential element of the mind-body-soul balance because it literally affects all three. Sacred texts throughout the ages have spoken of our bodies as vessels or temples that need to be honored and cared for. When we exercise, we display reverence for the magnificence of our bodies.

Find Your Rhythm

Discover the exercise that matches the rhythms of your day and the needs of your body. Be sure to breathe deeply as you move your muscles—oddly, many of us develop the habit of holding our breath as we lift a weight or swing a racket, depriving our muscles of much-needed oxygen.

Weave exercise into the fabric of your day: make a commitment to stretch whenever you get up from your desk, to choose the outer edges of every parking lot, to spend 10 minutes before bedtime practicing yoga. Find exercise that is fun for you: dancing, backpacking, even swinging on the swing set in your neighborhood park.

Don't let injuries or illnesses make you "give up" on exercise. Everyone can do some form of movement sitting in a chair, or even lying in bed. Simply breathing deeply and tensing and relaxing muscles can be immensely restorative. Turn on some music and move your body in whatever way feels comfortable. Start slowly and build up the amount of time you devote to movement each day.

Focus on pleasure, not pain. Exercise should feel *good*. If you don't look forward to your daily exercise, it's time to reexamine your choices. Release the idea that exercise has to be extremely vigorous, take an hour or more, and make you suffer. Studies show that three 10-minute increments of exercise spread throughout your day have the same health-giving benefits as one 30-minute session.

Exercise videos are a great way to sample a new discipline before you commit to taking a class. Some videos are broken down into short 10- or 20-minute segments to give you a quick lift when you're feeling out of balance. If you try something and you aren't enjoying it, try something else. Sample the wide variety of fun routines available and find the ones that restore and renew you. There are videos that give you instructions on how to exercise or do yoga in your bed, a chair, or an airplane seat. When you find something that clicks for you, you'll know it.

Make your choice: walk, swim, go to the gym, practice pilates, yoga, tai chi, chi gong . . . the list goes on and on. Move your body and bring a deeper, more satisfying balance to the rhythm of your days.

❧ ❧ ❧ ❧ ❧ ❧ ❧ ❧ ❧

ALTER Your Exercise

❧ ❧ ❧ ❧ ❧ ❧ ❧

ASK YOURSELF:

What kinds of exercise truly nourish me?

How can I add more movement to my day?

How can I bring variety to my daily exercise?

TELL YOURSELF:

"Breathe."

GIVE YOURSELF:

- a new yoga or pilates tape
- a two-minute stretch every time you get up from your desk
- the intention to view exercise not in terms of time or results, but in terms of pleasure and fulfillment

Shopping

ᴗ⸰ ᴗ⸰ ᴗ⸰ ᴗ⸰ ᴗ⸰ ᴗ⸰ ᴗ⸰ ᴗ⸰ ᴗ⸰ ᴗ⸰

Yesterday is a cancelled check; tomorrow is a promissory note;
today is the only cash you have—so spend it wisely.

~Kay Lyons

ᴗ⸰ ᴗ⸰ ᴗ⸰ ᴗ⸰ ᴗ⸰ ᴗ⸰ ᴗ⸰

THE MARKETPLACE HAS LONG BEEN the center of much more than simply the exchange of goods. Shopping calls us out of our isolation and loneliness into a sense of celebration and community. It can refresh us, entertain us, take our minds off of our troubles, give us a new take on life. It can be as profound as a holiday ritual, or as humble as the simple satisfaction of completing a necessary task.

Shopping can be transformative. You may need time away from your family, and shopping gives you a change of scenery and time alone with your thoughts. You may feel lonely, so you agree to meet an old friend you haven't seen in a long time and reconnect as you stroll, chat, and windowshop. You may not be in the mood for the holidays. But getting out to the stores and experiencing the music, decorations, and smiling faces lifts you out of your gloom. You may find yourself wearing that blue sweater, a gift from your ex, a little too often, and shopping for a new one to replace it may be the perfect ritual you need to let the relationship go.

Filling the Void

But of course there is a dark side to shopping today. The chaos of the modern marketplace has the potential to energize us, but often it overwhelms and overstimulates us. We are greeted at the door of the mega-mart with an avalanche of sights, sounds, and smells. We need a jar of mustard, but feel stymied by the fifty varieties lining the shelves: hot, sweet, or raspberry-infused? Imported, gourmet, or traditional? Jar or squeeze bottle? We buy things we don't need, or things we don't even want, and we stagger out into the parking lot feeling frazzled and drained, only to realize we failed to find the one item we truly needed.

Many of us shop in an attempt to fill an empty space in our lives—we crave *love*, so we buy *things*. The fun and exhilaration that can come from the shopping experience easily slips into a compulsion or addiction that no longer brings true pleasure, and instead damages our well-being, our relationships, and our finances. Bargain hunting becomes an obsessive quest—the search for the Holy Grail at 40 percent off—and we end up buying something not because it serves our authentic needs, but because "it was *on sale*."

We willingly swallow the cultural lie that ownership and accumulation of goods is the key to satisfaction and happiness, i.e. "the more you own, the happier you will be." The fact is, for many of us, shopping has taken on the form of a religion, and we are more likely to be found worshipping at the noisy altar of commerce than in a quiet chapel, temple, or mosque.

Shop but don't Drop

Begin to bring balance to your shopping experience by practicing mindfulness in the marketplace. Whether you purchase an apple, a sweater, or a washing machine, create a meaningful experience. Give thanks for the money you hold in your hand, for the abundance of goods to choose from, for the discernment to make wise purchases, for the people who assist you in the store.

Instead of mindlessly buying things to fill a void, consciously nurture your inner light by purchasing items that truly remind you of your childhood, make you feel safe, or express your unique personality. Be aware of your inner reactions and responses: if you feel enlivened, nurtured, and renewed by your shopping experience, you have struck a chord with your authentic self. If you feel exhausted, diminished, or guilty, chances are you are following the dictates of fear-based marketing, and are buying the item because you feel you "should", or because you think you will not "measure up" without it.

Delight in the opportunity that shopping provides to learn about diverse cultures. Few places are more deeply integrated in our society than the paths of commerce. Shopping can be an excellent learning opportunity where you can explore the nuances of handicraft, artistic expression, cultural bias, capitalism, or utilitarianism.

Revel in the sights and smells of a farmer's market, and give thanks for the people who grow the colorful fruits and vegetables that nourish you. Think of a clothing store as a museum, where you can observe and explore the art of design, the rich hues, innovative styles, and textured fabrics. Marvel in the creativity of these products. Your challenge is not to "shop 'til you drop," but to experience shopping as a playground of possibilities.

Getting and Spending

Practice the cleansing ritual of giving away possessions that no longer serve you. Make your life more a dance of "give and take" than "take and take and take."

In a global marketplace, every dollar you spend—or don't spend—is the equivalent of a vote for a certain future. Be aware of buying products associated with human rights abuses and environmental degradation. Patronize businesses that honor the well-being of their workers, their communities, and the planet.

It's true: money is power.

So use your power wisely.

⚘ ⚘ ⚘ ⚘ ⚘ ⚘ ⚘ ⚘ ⚘ ⚘

ALTER Your Shopping

⚘ ⚘ ⚘ ⚘ ⚘ ⚘ ⚘

ASK YOURSELF:

What do I truly enjoy about shopping?

Do I shop to fulfill real needs or emotional needs?

How can I make my everyday shopping trips more fulfilling?

TELL YOURSELF:

"I have everything I need."

GIVE YOURSELF:

- a goal to pay off one credit card
- a day trip antiquing with a friend
- permission to buy something that truly delights you

CHAPTER ELEVEN

Listening

ᘛᘛᘛᘛᘛᘛᘛᘛᘛᘛ

With the gift of listening comes the gift of healing.

~Catherine De Hueck

ᘛᘛᘛᘛᘛᘛᘛ

IN OUR CURRENT CULTURE, the gentle art of listening is not recognized as a skill—such as batting a baseball, or playing a violin—that requires awareness, intention, and practice in order to grow and develop. Rather, listening is often devalued as an act of passivity and weakness. We have become a sound-bite culture where verbal one-upmanship has overshadowed the grace and dignity of the humble and sacred practice of truly listening to what the other person is saying.

Faster, louder, stronger, we yak, yammer, and yell, but no one seems to be listening. Amid the frenzied cacophony of television and radio talk shows, silence—the foundation of all good listening—is often seen as a sign of stupidity or ignorance.

It may seem today's hectic world leaves little time to devote to the long-neglected art of listening. But if you pause for a moment and think about it, you will realize that adding this practice to your daily life literally takes no time at all.

Simply replace the time you used to spend mind*lessly not* listening with mind*fully* listening in silence and awareness, and you can instantly strengthen your ability to connect deeply to the magnificent human beings in your life. Truly listening can be a dynamic, powerful, even life-altering practice.

Hearing vs. Listening

A friend who has directed church choirs all his life remarked, "I have *heard* a lot of sermons in my life, but I have *listened* to only a few." Hearing is a passive act. It is the mechanical stimulation of auditory nerves in the ear by sound waves. Its primary evolutionary purpose is to alert us to danger.

Listening, on the other hand, is active: a skill that takes conscious practice and effort to develop fully. Just as you run scales on the piano or refine your backhand in tennis, listening skills will not develop without awareness, intention, and repetition.

Our minds tend to race as we drive, work, and even play. Intentional listening silences our inner chaos and calmly invites us back into the here and now. When we listen, we become a midwife, birthing something new in the heart of the person talking.

Have you ever surprised yourself by opening up intimately to a stranger simply because he or she was truly listening? Are there certain people who bring out the best in you by being a "good audience"? Commit today to being that type of person for everyone you see.

The Art of Listening

Listening is a sacred act of reverence. The skilled listener withholds judgment, and listens with an openness that expresses acceptance, vulnerability, and presence. Everyone we listen to becomes a special guest, invited into our personal inner sanctum. When we see listening as a gift that we can choose to give at any moment, it becomes the ultimate act of hospitality. And that gift is returned to us a hundredfold.

In the pure act and presence of listening, we give life to the experiences and words of others. Good listening demands the full presence of the listener. It requires an ability to enter into a deep silence even in a noisy environment. Silence is more than the absence of sound. Silence—the root of listening—is a profound connection to the essence of what it means to be human.

Listening *is* learning. The first thing we learn is what we've been missing by paying attention to the chatter in our heads instead of the people in our lives. Listening becomes our teacher as we learn the virtues of patience, stillness, and awareness. The awesome power of listening brings value, joy, and meaning into our lives.

Try consciously practicing listening with a friend or partner. Set a timer, and give each person 10 minutes to say whatever is on his or her mind while the other person practices deeply listening. You'll be surprised by what unfolds.

You give your loved ones a precious gift when you allow them to speak without spoiling their words with your own. Listening is the ultimate experience of relationship, a sacred entry into communion with another. When two connect to become one, the whole is truly greater than the sum of its parts.

⚘ ⚘ ⚘ ⚘ ⚘ ⚘ ⚘ ⚘ ⚘

ALTER Your Listening

⚘ ⚘ ⚘ ⚘ ⚘ ⚘ ⚘

ASK YOURSELF:

How can I deepen my listening
with the people in my lives?

Does my body language tell others I am listening?

What do I learn when I practice listening?

TELL YOURSELF:

"As I quiet my mind, I open my heart."

GIVE YOURSELF:

• ten minutes a day listening to a loved one

• an open heart as you listen

• an audiotape or CD of a inspirational text to
  listen to

CHAPTER TWELVE

Reading

⚹ ⚹ ⚹ ⚹ ⚹ ⚹ ⚹ ⚹ ⚹ ⚹

*You must understand the whole of life, not just one little part
of it. That is why you must read, that is why you must look
at the skies, that is why you must sing, and dance, and write
poems, and suffer, and understand, for all that is life.*

~Krishnamurti

⚹ ⚹ ⚹ ⚹ ⚹ ⚹ ⚹

WE ARE CURRENTLY EXPERIENCING a renewal of
our passion for reading. Oprah Winfrey opened the
door with her book club. The morning shows followed by plugging the hottest new titles. Bookstores are the latest
hip places to sip cappuccino and chat with like-minded people.

But what are we reading? It is important that we practice with
care what goes into our brain. In this age of information overload, we face the daily challenge of filtering out material that
insults our intelligence, exploits our emotions, depletes our creativity, and leaves us feeling as though we had just stuffed our
brains with junk food.

You alone are the gatekeeper for your mind. Choose reading
that challenges you, inspires you, nourishes you. Only you know
what kind of reading that is.

Trans-formative Reading

In our culture, we are trained to read for information and entertainment. We are taught to skim and scan for details, to engage in a critical dialog with the text. We have learned to sift, sort, question, and interact with the words as we read everything from the daily newspaper to murder mysteries.

A lesser-known approach to reading is called "formative reading," otherwise know as "reading for the soul." It is a time-honored path that can offer a balm to our overbusy lives, and it only takes slight shifts in *what* you read and *how* you read—not in how much time you spend reading.

Formative reading dwells on a text and its meaning. It is not a cognitive process, but an experiential one: it happens not in the mind, but the body, opening the reader to personal and communal transformation. When we read formatively, we go past the surface meaning of the words to experience the text as a whole, as a sacred work of art. This communion with another soul across time and space leads us to experience deeper and deeper levels of meaning and satisfaction.

Surrender

Our souls are tired and need nourishment. Our fast-paced world leaves us frazzled, drained, and exhausted. Formative reading can renew and refresh our world-weary souls. It can bring healing, depth, passion, and fresh perspectives to our lives.

The practice of formative reading has two simple elements: *trust* and *surrender*. Trust the author, and surrender to the text. Do not question or engage actively with the meaning. That can come later, if desired. Rather, surrender to the power of the words. Immerse yourself in their sound, feel, and texture. Absorb the words as if they were droplets of rain softly washing over you. Allow your depths to become touched and formed by the soul of the author.

Historically, humankind has practiced formative reading across all faiths and cultures. Sacred texts such as the Bible in Christianity, the Torah in Judaism, the Koran of Islam, the Upanishads and the Vedas in Hinduism, the Discourses of Buddha in Buddhism, the I Ching in Taoism, and the teachings of mystics throughout the ages all serve as a conduit for entering into a deeper communion with the unseen.

We can also practice formative reading with the great spiritual thinkers throughout history such as Thomas Merton, Henri Nouwen, or Anthony De Mello, or the noble poets and mystics of the ages, such as Rumi, Julian of Norwich, or St. Teresa of Avila. Find the text that resonates with your unique needs.

Words, Words, Words

As you allow the words of the text to surround and envelop you, read as though you have all the time in the world. Read passages that strike that inner chord over and over again. Each time you re-read a passage, it will sink deeper into you, and you will sink deeper into it. When you read the same passage at different times in your life, you re-experience the words from different perspectives, and discover different insights in the same text at different times and in different situations.

Read a poem or passage out loud and savor its sounds in your soul. Read a short passage, then put it down. Inhale. Exhale. Contemplate the message in silence. By breathing deeply and consciously, you strengthen neural connections, stimulate beneficial hormones, and invite in a profound sense of well-being.

Soak in the words. Let them permeate your whole body, lingering with you long after you have moved on from your reading. Practice awareness, intention, and choice to bring more balance and fulfillment to your everyday engagement with the written word.

⭑ ⭑ ⭑ ⭑ ⭑ ⭑ ⭑ ⭑ ⭑ ⭑

ALTER Your Reading

⭑ ⭑ ⭑ ⭑ ⭑ ⭑ ⭑

ASK YOURSELF:

"What kinds of books and magazines do I read?
What purpose do they serve in my life?"

"How can I fit more quality reading into my everyday life?"

"What life-altering books would I like to re-visit?"

TELL YOURSELF:

"I honor the power of the word."

GIVE YOURSELF:

- a small book of inspirational sayings
  on your desk

- ten minutes a day to read

- a subscription to a magazine that
  challenges your mind or spirit

ENERGY

Experience the Power

The Election

I WOKE UP IN THE DARK, startled by the sound of the telephone. Confused and somewhat disoriented, I couldn't recall how long I had been lying there. I didn't even make an attempt to answer the telephone as it continued to ring. The fact is it had been ringing for weeks. I hadn't been answering it, and every time I heard the ring, I shuddered inside.

My daughter opened my bedroom door, sat on the bed, kissed me gently on the cheek. "Mom, you've got to get up," she said. "You've got to eat something. Talk to me. Please, Mom. You're scaring me."

Just then, the phone rang again. Before I could stop her, my daughter reached for the phone and said, "Hello . . . yes, she is here, Mr. Landers. But she won't speak to anyone. She won't eat. She won't get out of bed." There was a silence and she said, "Mom, John Landers says if you don't talk to him on this phone right now, he is coming out here and dragging you out of that bed."

I buried my head in the pillow. "Tell him to go away."

My daughter, still on the phone, said to me, "He says you have thirty seconds to get on this phone or he is on his way."

I was panicked. I just wanted to move to another state. I wanted to disappear. I never wanted to be seen in public again. Not after what I had done. But I knew John, and if I didn't talk to him, he really would come out and drag me out of bed. Reluctantly, I took the call, a call that would give me the encouragement to release my shame and begin again.

Barely a year earlier, I was facilitating my regular cardiac wellness class at the local hospital, listening to my geriatric patients' worries about the enormous cost of prescription drugs. Some of them could hardly afford to eat and pay rent. The tremendous cost of health care and prescriptions were a continual topic of conversation at our group. The general public really doesn't appreciate how stressful it is for our older people to struggle with their day-to-day finances just to live. I listened to heartbreaking stories of these very real struggles for years.

One day an elderly patient said, "Dr. Hall, why don't you run for office and help us? You understand what we go through. We would all help you if you would run for the legislature." The rest of the group chimed in, encouraging me to be their voice at the capitol. At first I shrugged the offer off, but that night I tossed and turned, unable to put it out of my mind. I knew nothing about politics. I had never run for any office in my life. I had worked with the disadvantaged, the poor, the sick, and the disabled for many years, and felt confident in that field. But I never considered running for office and becoming a politician.

I had seen firsthand the powerlessness in poverty and aging. I surely had a handle on what many people needed and what was missing in their lives, but I never considered throwing my hat into the political arena. It was a bizarre thought to me.

Maybe I could run for office, I thought. I had just earned my doctorate. I was educated, passionate, had an inordinate amount of energy, and loved people. But then the dark inner personal fears started clamoring. What if I lost? How embarrassing would it be to lose in front of 50,000 people? How would I live with the rejection? And, as a progressive woman running in the rural North Georgia Mountains, did I really have a chance?

Many people in the county began quietly building support for my candidacy. Before I knew it, people were calling and asking me to make it official. The night before official notice of candidacy was due at the capitol in Atlanta, my stomach was in knots as I tried to decide which choice to make. I sat on my back porch, watching the horses graze in the pasture as the sun was setting.

I imagined I was eighty years old, sitting in that same rocking chair, my granddaughter sitting at my feet, asking, "Grandma, what was the best thing you ever did in your life?"

I saw myself smiling at her, answering, "Honey, once a group of citizens asked me to represent them in the state legislature, and I said yes. I was afraid I'd lose and be embarrassed. But

Susie, I ran for that office. I risked everything and ran. That was the greatest thing I ever did."

Then I imagined that I was eighty years old, sitting in that same rocking chair on that same porch, and my granddaughter asked, "Grandma, what was the worst thing you ever did in your life?"

I saw myself wrinkling my brow and frowning as I answered, "Honey, once a group of citizens asked me to represent them in the state legislature, and I said no. I was afraid that I would lose and be embarrassed. I will always wonder if I would have won, always wonder how it would have effected my life and the lives of others."

I woke up the next morning, drove to Atlanta, and registered to run for the Georgia legislature. It was an amazing experience. My loving, loyal cardiac, pulmonary, and cancer patients were my volunteers for the election. It was such a blessing to see my campaign headquarters loaded with devoted workers. Some campaigned on walkers, some in wheelchairs, some pulling oxygen tanks behind them. They worked all day and night stuffing envelopes, answering telephones, and campaigning around the community in bright red t-shirts that read, "Kathleen Hall 2000."

I soon learned a lot about the dark side of politics. Right after the campaign started, my opponent approached me before a debate, shook my hand, and said, "Don't take what I say and do personally." I stared at him, shocked at his ominous warning. A week later, a seasoned politician sitting beside me at a fundraiser whispered in my ear, "Now that you are running for political office, you will really learn what hate is." I will never forget the chill that went up my spine.

Well, I lost the election. But I walked through many great fears along the campaign trail, and learned a lot about the nature of power in politics and government. Above all, I learned one of the most valuable lessons in my life that year: that even by running and losing, I could win. I experienced what real community is: giving, sharing, loyalty, laughter, crying, and total commitment to each other and a common cause.

I now know thousands of people I never would have known. Every time I go to the local supermarket or Wal-Mart, people still come up to me, shake my hand and tell me they voted for me, or spent hours putting signs up for me, or spent a night baking cookies for a fundraiser. Running for political office was a profound spiritual experience and a lesson in humility. A public loss is a wonderful lesson in humility—and love.

I entered the political arena mindful of the power of choice. I promised to do every thing in my power to win the election, and to surrender to the painful lessons I might have to learn in the process. We all suffer loss in our life, and often our most valuable and profound life lessons come to us through loss. When we choose to live an intentional life we become aware that we have the power to choose our response to our losses and suffering.

Remember that phone call I took from John Landers back when my wounds were still deep? That day, John told me to come to our Rotary meeting, or he would drag me to it. I told him I was too embarrassed to show my face in public. John said he would be proud to walk into Rotary with me, proud that I ran an ethical, honest race. He assured me that getting 40% of the vote against a long-entrenched incumbent was an amazing accomplishment.

When I chose to run for the legislature, I had no idea of the lessons I would learn, the people whose lives I would touch, and the people whose lives would touch mine. Each choice we make, moment by moment, has an unseen ripple effect on the entire world.

The Bishop

I walked into my class in seminary at Emory with great anticipation: Nobel Peace Prize winner Bishop Desmond Tutu was my teacher. I expected him to be a large, tall, and strong man who walked in a deliberate, powerful manner—literally larger than life. From what I had read about this man, he was almost a Christ-like figure, to be honored and revered.

But that day in class a tiny man stood at the front of the room. How could this little man—with an infectious laugh that could melt your heart—have had such a powerful effect on the world? I would learn that it was his smile, his voice, and his boundless love for humankind.

I can still hear his voice—passionate, heartbreaking, pleading, soft, loving, tender, compassionate and holy. When I close my eyes, the image of his angelic face appears before me. He has a look that can make you cry, smile, and tremble. It's an indescribable experience when you know you are in the presence of a great soul.

It has been one of the greatest privileges in my life to have personally experienced the holiness of this man. I can still hear his laughter echoing in my soul. Bishop Tutu's life is a model of an intentional life. He has witnessed torture, slaughter and other atrocities on an unimaginable scale, but never once has he responded with hatred, revenge, or retribution.

One morning, a student in our class asked him how he could not despise the racists, the hatemongers, and the murderers he encountered in South Africa. How did he deal with the hate and violence? Bishop Tutu answered, "I do not see black, nor white, just Christ in all people." Then he told a story to illustrate his point.

Early one morning Bishop Tutu was awoken by banging on his door. A young boy from the village school told him the boys at the school planned a march to the sea at sunrise to touch the ocean with their own hands. At this time under apartheid, blacks were not allowed to use the beaches, and the white army used gunfire to enforce the laws.

But these young boys were determined to bring the injustice of this law to light by courageously marching en masse to the sea that morning. The boy who woke Bishop Tutu was afraid there would be violence and hoped that the Bishop could convince the boys to cancel their plans. Bishop Tutu rushed to the school, only to find the boys lined up and ready to march to the sea.

The army knew of the boy's plan for the march and was waiting for them. Bishop Tutu begged them to go back to their homes and stop the march, but the boys said they would not be stopped. So arm in arm the young boys marched to the sea. Bishop Tutu knew the only hope of stopping the violence was to accompany the boys on the march and be their spokesperson. He joined the boys as they headed for the sea. As they reached the sea, they faced a formation of armed soldiers lined up to keep the young boys from advancing.

A young white lieutenant approached and said, "Bishop Tutu, you must turn these boys back to the village. You know they are not allowed to go to the beach." Bishop Tutu pleaded with the lieutenant, as he watched the other soldiers, rifles loaded, waiting for orders.

The lieutenant was becoming increasingly nervous, beads of sweat streaming down his narrow sallow face, as he pleaded with Bishop Tutu one last time, "Bishop, I will have to give the order to open fire on the boys if they march on to the sea."

Bishop Tutu held the lieutenant's head gently in his hands, looked deeply into his blue eyes, and said that he understood he had orders and he understood what he must do. Nevertheless, he would continue to lead the boys to the ocean. "I ask that you shoot me first," he told the lieutenant, "And when you shoot me, know that I love you. Know that I forgive you." Then he kissed the lieutenant on the cheek and smiled.

Bishop Tutu noticed that the lieutenant was pale, sweaty and shaking. He took the hands of the boys and began the final steps across the sand to the sea. As he turned his back on the soldiers and began to walk away, he heard the lieutenant call the order, "Take your aim, ready . . ." Then there was silence—a deafening silence that seemed to last an eternity.

He turned around and saw the lieutenant drop his rifle and fall to the sand weeping. Bishop Tutu let go of the boys' arms and walked back to the Lieutenant. He bent down, wiped away the lieutenant's tears, and said, "I love you, my son." As those words left his mouth, he could hear the joyful screams and laughter of the boys as they raced to the beach and splashed the water of the ocean at each other. Bishop Tutu held the lieutenant, comforting him as he breathed a sigh of relief.

Holy courageous people like Bishop Tutu walk among us and live lives of passion and power each and every day. Yes, they do great things—great things maybe you and I are not prepared to do yet. But I promise you this: each of them started out on a path to live an intentional life by doing the smallest of things.

They continually experience energy in the simplest acts of life. Authentic power requires action. Choosing to live an intentional life invites your participation to become active in social justice for the entire human family.

When you first become aware of the energy and power you experience from living an intentional life, a challenge immediately emerges. Can you choose to surrender to each new life circumstance, and in that surrender experience infinite possibilities, not problems? Or, will you choose to seek only certain kinds of experiences and deny, exclude and isolate anything that my make you feel uncomfortable?

Consider the small choices we make, often mindlessly, every day. By bringing intention and awareness to each moment and listening to that still voice deep within, we can make even ordinary moments—such as walking the dog, weeding the garden, or washing the dishes—extraordinary moments of fulfillment and renewal.

CHAPTER THIRTEEN

Animals

❧ ❧ ❧ ❧ ❧ ❧ ❧ ❧ ❧ ❧

"I think I could turn and live with the animals,
they are so placid and self-contain'd.
I stand and look at them long and long.
They do not sweat and whine about their condition,
They do not lie awake in the dark and weep for their sins,
They do not make me sick discussing their duty to God,
Not one is dissatisfied, not one is demented
with the mania of owning things,
Not one kneels to another, nor to his kind
that lived thousands of years ago,
Not one is respectable or unhappy over
the whole earth."

~Walt Whitman

❧ ❧ ❧ ❧ ❧ ❧ ❧

EVEN BEFORE THE WRITTEN WORD EXISTED, human beings communicated their profound connection with animals through petroglyphs drawn on cave walls, in textile and pottery design, in carvings and statues. Throughout history, humankind has shared a practical, mystical, and profound relationship with animals: they have been, and continue to be, our beloved guardians, partners, mentors, and guides.

But increasing urbanization has separated us from our traditional intimate interaction with animals. We no longer mark our mornings by milking the cow, our evenings by feeding the chickens. Our modern environment is so visually stimulating that we often don't even pause to notice the squirrel spiraling up a tree or the bird resting on the wire. Sadly, when we are disconnected from animals, we become disconnected from ourselves, for human beings are part of the natural world, not separate from it.

But there is evidence that we are experiencing a renewal of respect for animals in our culture. We are beginning to acknowledge that our health and well-being, even our survival, depends on our relationship with animals. Throughout the country, state and local governments are enacting new laws that protect animals from abuse and neglect and provide strict punishments for those who violate these laws. The deep ecology movement shows we are awakening to the reality that a profound respect for animals and our environment is necessary for the well-being of our planet. The measure of a society is how it treats its animals.

Our Four-Footed Friends

Daily connection to animals promotes our mental, emotional, and physical well-being. Modern science tells us what many of us have known all along: that relating to animals has a powerful healing effect. Sharing your life with a four-footed friend can lower blood pressure, lower cholesterol, and ward off depression. Elderly patients who have animal companions visit doctors less often than those without pets, and Alzheimer's patients are shown to have fewer outbursts when there is an animal in the home.

Living with a dog or cat improves survival rates after heart attack, and even cuts down on the number of visits to the doctor. The scientific data is so convincing that Midland Life Insurance Company gives elderly pet owners preferential treatment when they are looking for life or long-term-care insurance.

Animals are going with us into nursing homes and hospitals to facilitate healing. They are used therapeutically to treat a wide variety of disorders, from autism to post traumatic stress syndrome. There are also those that work for a living; drug dogs, bomb dogs, cadaver dogs, seeing-eye dogs and seeing-eye ponies provide huge benefits to their human companions. When we surrender to the lessons they have to teach us, animals will lead us on a rich and profound journey into a way of knowing beyond words.

Listen to the Animals

Writer Eckhart Tolle remarks, "I have studied under many excellent Zen masters, most of whom were cats." From ancient Egyptians to the modern-day Buddhists, a wide array of traditions honor animals as mystical creatures who share a quiet wisdom with those who are ready to listen. In Native American and other shamanic traditions, animals are experienced as totems—powerful archetypes with attributes that can be called upon for power and assistance: the deer for gentleness, the dog for loyalty, the horse for power, the eagle for spirit, the butterfly for transformation.

Many of us experience animals as the presence of angels in our midst; they comfort us when we are sick and hurting, cheer us when we are sad and lonely. Animals model virtues we often only experience in the realms of saints as they model humility, loyalty, unselfishness, forgiveness, happiness, playfulness, unconditional love, and a profound sense of inner peace. Just by being who they are, animals remind us to lighten up and enjoy the simple pleasures every day brings.

None of us can forget the pure, simple, but amazingly powerful experience of sharing life with our first pets. Our first childhood experience of the natural cycles of life and death often came through our relationships with our animal friends, and they often gave us our first lessons in friendship, kindness, gentleness, and responsibility as well.

A pet has an amazing power to ground you and bring you into the present moment—a dog or a cat doesn't fret over the past or fear the future, but lives solely, joyfully in the now. Animals invite us to explore, enjoy, and integrate our animal natures—a vital part of ourselves we rarely acknowledge or give credence to.

When you greet your pet, look intentionally into his or her eyes, smile, and be grateful for his or her contribution to your daily life. Practice blessing your pet in whichever way seems natural to you—through a word, a gift, or a ritual. Be creative with your good wish for your companion. Make sure you give thanks to your pet for his or her life and sharing your journey together. Notice how this simple practice brings you more fully into the present. You will come to love this practice, and so will your beloved pet.

Animals remind us each day of the simple joy of being alive. They remind us that we are never alone, but part of the larger interconnected community of all life in this world.

꙳ ꙳ ꙳ ꙳ ꙳ ꙳ ꙳ ꙳ ꙳ ꙳

ALTER Your Relationship with Animals

꙳ ꙳ ꙳ ꙳ ꙳ ꙳ ꙳

ASK YOURSELF:

"Why do I, or why don't I have a pet?"

"How can I bring more quality to the time I spend with animals?"

"What can I learn from the animals in my life?"

TELL YOURSELF:

"Animals support and guide my journey through life"

GIVE YOURSELF:

- a bird feeder by your favorite window

- time each day to relax with your animal

- sponsorship of a cause that supports animals

CHAPTER FOURTEEN

Gardening

༅ ༅ ༅ ༅ ༅ ༅ ༅ ༅ ༅ ༅

"Cultivate peace and harmony."
~George Washington

༅ ༅ ༅ ༅ ༅ ༅ ༅

GARDENING HAS BEEN AN INTEGRAL PART of the human experience since we first sowed wheat by the Tigris and Euphrates eight thousand years ago. The ancient tombs of the pharaohs were painted with murals of life-giving crops. In Europe, explorers kept detailed records of the plants found in their travels, and brought back fruits and vegetables from the new lands across the seas. Seeds were considered sacred and were handed down from generation to generation like valuable jewels. As we settled new lands, one of the most precious objects we carried with us were our seeds.

There is a tremendous reverence for plants and gardens in the early teachings of all cultures and faiths. From mud huts to monasteries to palaces, all of humanity cultivated gardens that connected them to the Divine. Our peace and vitality is inextricably linked to growing things.

But since the Industrial Revolution, we have methodically become more and more disconnected from the earth. We now pick our beans off the shelf at the local megamart instead off the vine in the field. Corporate agriculture and the institutionalization of food production has separated us from our profoundly deep connection to the earth and her wisdom. Perhaps as a result of this separation, in recent years we have been showing an almost revolutionary return to a more reverent relationship with the earth. Even the most urban markets now feature local and organic produce, and gourmet restaurants work with local growers to provide fresh seasonal greens for salads. We place fresh flowers in our homes and plants in our offices. The popularity of nature-centered practices such as bonsai, ikebana, and feng shui are bringing the art of the garden back into our popular culture.

The Garden as Classroom

For many, the Garden of Eden was the birthplace of the human race. Buddha taught his followers in the garden under a bodhi tree. Jesus taught his disciples outdoors, and prayed for guidance in the Garden of Gethsemane. Hindus still worship their gods with gifts from the earth. As Thich Nhat Hanh says, "Earth brings us into life and nourishes us. Earth takes us back again. Birth and death are present in every moment."

The metaphors for a balanced life are grounded in gardening: scattering seed, planting, watering, nurturing, growing, harvesting, storing. Gardening connects us to the natural cycles of the seasons: the new life of spring, the abundance of summer, the shedding and surrender of fall, the peace and stillness of winter. And gardening also connects us to the natural cycles of life and death: the seed is given life by the earth; is nourished by sunlight, rain, and minerals; it sprouts, grows, blooms; and then returns to the earth in its death, leaving new seed for regeneration and rebirth.

Gardening leads us to the sacred practice of tending. We feel awe and reverence for the amazing potential of a small seed. We practice trust and surrender as we drop a seed into the dark mysteries of the soil. We practice patience, perseverance, and daily responsibility. We learn profound lessons about loss, hope, joy, gratitude, success, and failure. We witness the life cycle arising from and returning to Mother Earth. We experience the interconnectedness of all life.

The balance of the elements in a garden reflects the balance in your own life. A garden leads you into the experience of trust because you are trusting in the life cycle—the cycle of Nature. As this trust develops, your reverence for your connection to the earth continues to grow.

Your Green Thumb

Gardening is a rich exercise in awareness. Practice awareness with the growing things in your life: do they need water? light? nutrients? By connecting more deeply to your garden, you connect more deeply to your inner self and your relation to the world around you. Gardening invites you into the present moment—the sun on your back, the rich earth crumbling beneath your spade, the miracle of the first tiny green shoots. Gardening provides an easy everyday opportunity to experience the fullness of joy, peace, and serenity.

Nothing is more safe, delicious, and good for you than food grown on your own land. But you don't necessarily have to have a large garden like our grandparents did in years past. "Container gardening" is a simple and fun way to bring the wonders of nature into even the most urban environment. Try a tomato or flower for your patio or yard, or small pots of herbs on your balcony. Experience the process of growth and change and see how it reflects in your life.

Even though nutritionists recommend fresh fruit and vegetables as a mainstay in our diet and a source of vital anti-oxidants, most Americans don't get the recommended seven daily servings of fruits and vegetables. Does this disconnection from our natural diet reflect our overall disconnection from nature? See if you can bring more healthy fruits and vegetables into your daily life. Hold an orange in your hands and smell it before you peel it. Be mindful of where it came from, of how the tree created the orange from earth, air, sunlight, and water. Notice the miraculous texture of the fruit, wonder at the fragrant oils that pop off the rind as you peel it, and savor its juicy flavor as you renew your connection to the earth in the most ordinary moments of your day.

Many of us live in urban areas or our lives are too busy to tend a large garden. But you can still experience the thrill of gardening by purchasing plants and fresh fruits and vegetables on a regular basis. The local fresh-air farmer's market or garden center can become your surrogate garden. Or create a mini-garden by putting a plant in your kitchen window, by your bathtub, on your desk, or slip a flower in a bud vase in your car. The simplest gestures can connect you back to the earth, your mother.

✢ ✢ ✢ ✢ ✢ ✢ ✢ ✢ ✢ ✢

ALTER Your Gardening

✢ ✢ ✢ ✢ ✢ ✢ ✢

ASK YOURSELF:

In what ways can I connect with the earth in my daily life?

What memories do I have of gardens in my life?

What plants am I attracted to?

TELL YOURSELF:

"My life is my garden."

GIVE YOURSELF:

- a live plant in your office
- the commitment to plant something and watch it grow
- a book or class about a flower or plant you love

CHAPTER FIFTEEN

Leisure

৯৮ ৯৮ ৯৮ ৯৮ ৯৮ ৯৮ ৯৮ ৯৮ ৯৮ ৯৮

"One day a hunter in the desert saw Abba Anthony enjoying himself with the brethren and he was shocked. What kind of spiritual guide was this? But the old monk said to him, 'Put an arrow in your bow and shoot it.' So the hunter did. Then the old man said, 'Now shoot another.' And the hunter did. Then the elder said, 'Shoot your bow again. Keep shooting; keep shooting; keep shooting.' And the hunter finally said, 'But if I bend my bow so much I will break it.'

Then Abba Anthony said to him, 'It is just the same with the work of God. If we stretch ourselves beyond measure, we will break. Sometimes it is necessary to meet other needs.' When the hunter heard these words he was struck with remorse and, greatly edified by Anthony, he went away. As for the monastics there, they went home strengthened."

~The Desert Fathers

৯৮ ৯৮ ৯৮ ৯৮ ৯৮ ৯৮ ৯৮

EVEN AS EARLY AS THE SECOND CENTURY, Abba Anthony cautioned his followers not to forget the critical role of leisure in a balanced life. Nineteen centuries later, we need to follow his wise advice more than ever. Traditionally, the natural cycles of day and night provided a framework for the balance of work and leisure, but with the advent of electricity and artificial light sources, we can and do continue to work later and later into the night, throwing our natural cycles out of balance, wearying our bodies and drying up our souls.

Chinese philosopher Lin Yutang observes that ". . . the most bewildering thing about man is his idea of work and the amount of work he imposes upon himself, or civilization has imposed upon him. All nature loafs, while man alone works for a living." Americans have forgotten how to exercise the power of choice in the types and amount of work they do. Priding ourselves on being the hardest working nation in the world, we glorify work and workaholics to the point where workaholism is the most socially sanctioned and encouraged addiction we have. This narrow vision has thrust our society terribly out of balance. Remember seesaw on the playground? Balance depends upon an equal portion of work and leisure.

The Soul of Leisure

Even though leisure is essential to our well-being, we often devalue and dismiss our need for unstructured time because our culture encourages us to be doers and builders, not dreamers and reflectors. Productivity and self-sacrifice are rewarded, and reflection and renewal are discouraged.

The practice of the Sabbath, or a day of rest, is part of all major world religions. The Sabbath is not just a story about God needing rest; it is meant to teach *us* to rest. The Talmud teaches that honoring the Sabbath equalizes rich and poor, gives us time to evaluate our work to see if it is good; and gives us leisure to contemplate the meaning of life.

When we take time away from work, our work ceases to define us, and artificial measures of status fall away as we see we share common spaces and activities with people from all walks of life. When we take time to contemplate our work and our role in the world, we readjust our internal compasses as we travel the road of an intentional life. And when we stop to explore our role in the big picture, we renew our energy and connection to the Divine. Leisure engages the heart and stretches the soul.

In the book of Genesis, after completing the work of creation, God stopped and rested from all work—and then "blessed and sanctified" the day. Every day should have some "blessed and sanctified" time, just as every week should have such a day, and each year a substantial period of time away from work for rest, renewal, and reflection.

On the Playground of Life

Leisure has two aspects: rest and play. Isn't it sad that in our society we teach everyone to work, but we don't teach anyone how to play? Play has been the basis of leisure time throughout all societies. Traditional holy days and festivals provided all socioeconomic and social classes of people the opportunity to play and celebrate together.

We often think of leisure as a time to "escape" from life, but true leisure pulls us deeper into life by allowing time for dreaming and contemplation, which are at the root of all creative acts. Leisure is essential to the health and happiness of the human race. Work becomes more meaningful and has more purpose when we take regular breaks to play and rest.

Now is the time to explore and discover new ways to play and to rest. Be creative. Explore new possibilities. Make it fun. There are many opportunities that you may not be aware of: museum openings, art festivals, free concerts, zoos, historical sites. The internet is a great resource for finding current activities in your neighborhood.

For your rest time, take a nap. Even a ten-minute nap can be immensely restorative. Or sit on the ground and rest against a tree like you did when you were a child. Lie on your back in your yard or in a park and rediscover the animal shapes hiding in the clouds. Rediscover your inner child on the playground of life and never, ever lose that vital joy again.

❊ ❊ ❊ ❊ ❊ ❊ ❊ ❊ ❊ ❊

ALTER Your Leisure

❊ ❊ ❊ ❊ ❊ ❊ ❊

ASK YOURSELF:

Am I playful? If not, why not?

How do I feel about leisure time?

How can I bring more leisure time into my life?

TELL YOURSELF:

"I discover new energy when I play and rest."

GIVE YOURSELF:

- scheduled leisure time each week
- a nice restorative nap
- carefree playtime with your loved ones

CHAPTER SIXTEEN

Music

≫ ≫ ≫ ≫ ≫ ≫ ≫ ≫ ≫

If you cannot teach me to fly, teach me to sing.

~Sir James Barrie

≫ ≫ ≫ ≫ ≫ ≫ ≫

MUSIC IS THE MOST GENUINE, flawless, and authentic form of communication we have, as its magic bypasses the brain and goes straight to the heart. Music communicates far more than mere words, and is not dependent on language to be understood. Music transcends cultural, economic, and social barriers; it is the common language of the human family that connects us intimately to each other across time and space.

Some of the earliest music, such as drumming and horns, was used to communicate across distances, to warn of invaders or celebrate special events. In a wide variety of cultures drumming and chanting is used as a vehicle for earth-bound humans to travel to heavenly realms, and choral music is used for communal lamentation, praise, and thanksgiving. Music can connect us more deeply to ourselves and our communities, and can connect us to a presence greater than ourselves.

Reasons Behind Rhythms

A Michigan State University study shows that listening to music for only fifteen minutes increases the blood's level of Interluken-1—a family of proteins associated with blood and platelet production and cellular protection against AIDS, cancer, and many other diseases. *The Journal of the American Medical Association* reports that half of the mothers who listen to music during childbirth do not require anesthesia. Music is used in hospitals and nursing homes to soothe the anxious and lull the restless to sleep.

Corporations have found that music can be used in the workplace to increase efficiency, cut training time, and increase output; one study shoes that a group of workers listening to music increased productivity over 21 percent. Restaurants have long used music to provide a friendly environment that will give their patrons a positive dining experience and stimulate digestion.

Music has an immediate effect on our emotions: it stimulates the pituitary gland and increases levels of endorphins, the brain's natural "feel good" chemicals, thereby alleviating fatigue and mild depression. A scientist at Stanford found in a recent study that half his subjects experienced euphoria while listening to music. Consider the ways you can use music in your life to boost your productivity, increase your energy, or relax and restore your body.

Who Could Ask for Anything More?

Music is a medium that breaks down cultural barriers and allows us to communicate without the hindrance of language differences. Even if we do not know the meaning of the words being sung, we can "feel" the message on a level beyond words. Music is also culturally defined. We may be in Asia, South America, or Africa and know immediately where we are by the music being played. Think about Disney's Epcot Center, where they indicate what "nation" you are visiting simply by changing the soundtrack!

Music invites you to explore the mystery that dances within your soul. Be aware of what types of music "speak to you" and what types of music drain you. Broaden your music life by exploring different forms of music or music from other cultures. Explore the spiritual side of music. You may want to visit a drumming circle, sing in a choir, or take lessons on an instrument you played as a child.

If you have always wanted to sing and have never felt comfortable with your voice, release your internal judgments, have a karaoke night, and sing your heart out. Or put music on that you love in your car and sing along. Like the birds, we are all meant to sing. Singing has a powerful ability to stimulate respiration and circulation, express repressed emotions, and transport you to a higher dimension.

⚹ ⚹ ⚹ ⚹ ⚹ ⚹ ⚹ ⚹ ⚹ ⚹

ALTER Your Music

⚹ ⚹ ⚹ ⚹ ⚹ ⚹ ⚹

ASK YOURSELF:

Do I listen to music often? If not, why not?

What types of music do I love?

What different types of music would I like to explore?

TELL YOURSELF:

"Music inspires my mind, body and soul."

GIVE YOURSELF:

- a CD or tape from a new and different band or artist

- five or ten minutes a day listen to music

- time at least once a day to sing

CHAPTER SEVENTEEN

Dinner

⚹ ⚹ ⚹ ⚹ ⚹ ⚹ ⚹ ⚹ ⚹ ⚹

One cannot think well, love well, sleep well, if one has not dined well.

~Virginia Woolf

⚹ ⚹ ⚹ ⚹ ⚹ ⚹ ⚹

W**E HAVE FORGOTTEN THE TRUE MEANING** of the world "feast." Many of us experience our evening meal as a mundane event, or simply another exhausting task at the end of an already overwhelming day. Dining has been relegated to a prefabricated ritual that has lost all its reverence in our consumer society with all its modern conveniences. Many of us experience our daily meals as fast food, take-out food, food in a bag, box, or can, dehydrated food, frozen food, instant food. When the way we experience food becomes routine and institutionalized, we have to be careful that we do not lose the reverence for the sacred process that put the food on our tables, and suffer a separation from Mother Nature herself, thereby separating ourselves from our source of energy and renewal.

The current trend of remodeling kitchens and filling them with gadgets and gizmos is our attempt to reconnect with times past, when the kitchen was the heart of the home. We all yearn to reclaim the comfort and joy of eating and cooking in the kitchens of our mothers and grandmothers. The kitchen is the new living room, the social area of the home, the primary entertainment venue for the home. It is the place where family, holiday and religious rituals are celebrated. Intimate conversations are carried deep into the night with the hearts and souls of those gathered there inextricably woven together.

Technology has blessed us with convenience, but we must be cautious that this does not drive us further and further away from our grounding in the earth. The core of the human experience, the foundation of our drive to do productive work, is the transformation of raw ingredients into mental, physical, emotional and spiritual nourishment and sustenance. It is time to reclaim this basic connection.

Return to the Sacred

All spiritual traditions share the feast ritual. Judaism has Shabbat and Seder; Christianity has Holy Communion. Islam celebrates the Feast of Eid Al-Fitr, marking the end of the fast of Ramadan. In Buddhism and Taoism, reverence is shown for the gods through food offerings. Hindus feed their gods fruits, milk, and nuts. There are countless meals throughout the various faiths associated with holidays, rites, and rituals.

Religious traditions also have customs about the types of foods consumed and the methods by which food is prepared. Catholicism historically excluded the partaking of meat on

Fridays and certain holy days. Traditionally, Jews eat kosher food that is prepared according to a code of strict dietary laws that provide, among other things, that meat and dairy products must be prepared separately and must not be eaten together. Buddhists do not generally eat meat at all. And where many Hindus avoid beef, neither Muslims nor Jews consume pork. Whatever the practice, dietary restrictions teach us reverence, gratitude, and discipline, and deepen our connection to our heritage and our faith.

In many cultures there is an emphasis on intention and emotion in cooking. The simplest meal can be the healthiest food in the world if prepared in a spirit of affection and goodwill. A happy loving cook is seen to strengthen the nourishing and healing power of each dish. The *Bhagavad Gita*—a sacred Hindu scripture—teaches that the intention of the cook is actually transferred to the food.

The Mindful Feast

Rediscover the authentic joy of preparing and sharing food by choosing to *be* in the kitchen, not just *do* in the kitchen. Challenge yourself and your loved ones to eat intentionally at least once a week. Don't just gobble down a chocolate cake, but revel in the wonderful process of preparing it, from breaking the eggs to mixing the ingredients to licking the beaters. If you live with others, it is important to have times together to prepare the family meal. Invite friends and neighbors on the spur of the moment for a pot-luck gathering; every meal doesn't have to be formal and impressive. If you live alone, attempt to share a meal once a week with someone, a friend or a neighbor, and maybe even consider creating a meal-time family.

Develop mindfulness in your cooking. Tap into your creativity by exploring the different colors, textures, and origins of foods. There has never been a better time for making food choices. Consider where your food is grown. Is your food home-grown? Is it organic? Part of the practice of reverence for food is making intelligent decisions about your food choices.

Don't feel like you are short-changing your family if you choose vegetables that are frozen or easily prepared; not all of us have the access to specialty markets or the time to prepare every meal from scratch. Companies like Bird's Eye have developed techniques that capture more of the nutritional value of the food, and the larger companies are beginning to respond to their customers' needs for foods that are free of pesticides and other chemicals. National growers meet tough standards for food quality from the FDA.

Attempt to make at least an occasional dinner a time for a true feast. Turn off the television, the computer, and the phone. Pull out the family silver, the linen napkins, the good china. Light candles and put fresh flowers on your table.

Develop dinnertime rituals that speak to your soul. Create your own unique personal blessing that acknowledges the process by which your food came to your table, your gratefulness for the sacrifices others have made for your meal, and your gratitude for being blessed with enough to eat. Begin your meal by taking three deep breaths, pausing and looking at your food, and practicing gratitude. Appreciate the colors, textures, and aromas while you consider all the work and wonder that went into this meal. Connect in silence with the people gathered, and enjoy the peace and fellowship of a leisurely feast.

When eating becomes a mindful process, you begin to develop a healthier relationship with your food, bringing better balance to your meals. Taking a few extra intentional minutes at meal time is one of the easiest ways to turn an everyday activity into a fulfilling and rewarding experience.

❧ ❧ ❧ ❧ ❧ ❧ ❧ ❧ ❧ ❧

ALTER Your Dinner

❧ ❧ ❧ ❧ ❧ ❧ ❧

ASK YOURSELF:

Do I eat mindfully now?

What would I like to change about dinner?

I just read many suggestions: which would I like to follow?

TELL YOURSELF:

"My meal nourishes me in every way."

GIVE YOURSELF:

- one traditional meal a week with your loved ones

- time on the weekend to plan the weekly meals

- new linens, china, or crystal that you love

CHAPTER EIGHTEEN

Washing the Dishes

⚹ ⚹ ⚹ ⚹ ⚹ ⚹ ⚹ ⚹ ⚹ ⚹

Confine yourself to the present.

~Marcus Aurelius

⚹ ⚹ ⚹ ⚹ ⚹ ⚹ ⚹

WHAT TASK COULD BE MORE ORDINARY and everyday than washing the dishes? For many of us, it is the standard family punishment, or a begrudging trade-off for not cooking. In truth, washing the dishes is a profound part of the cycle of rituals we have around food. If you don't finish the dishes, you are not completing the cycle, which is necessary in order to start the ritual again.

Holy Dishwashers

Brother Lawrence was a Carmelite monk who lived in France during the seventeenth century. His spiritual counsel was simple: throughout every day, keep an ongoing conversation with God. He joyfully scrubbed the pots of his monastery in order to see the face of God in his reflection under the grime of the day's meal. Modern Buddhist monk Thich Nhat Hanh uses washing dishes as an opportunity to practice prayer and meditation.

Transform the time you ordinarily spend washing to dishes into an opportunity to practice awareness, mindfulness, and inner calm. It takes only re-affirmation of your commitment to living an intentional life to turn the fifteen minutes you ordinarily spend doing dishes into a joyful and restorative meditative experience rather than an exhausting task. Instead of the time being hurried and unpleasant, choose to focus on your breath, listen to music, sing, or chant. Notice the delicate patina on the silver, the tiny flowers at the edge of plate. Give thanks for the simple vessels that we use to hold our food.

Wash Away the Blues

Revel in the sensual renewal of warm water on your hands and steam in your face, the down-to-earth pleasure that comes from completing a humble task. Consider the miracle of indoor plumbing: the incredible gift of hot and cold running water only a small percentage of the earth's inhabitants enjoy.

The metaphor of cleansing, of washing away the traces of the past, strikes a deep chord in our souls. No matter how little control we may seem to have over the other aspects of our lives, completing everyday tasks gives us a feeling of accomplishment, the simple joy that comes from tidying up one small part of our world. If you are anxious, allow the ritual to calm you. If you are angry or frustrated, express your excess emotional energy by scrubbing pots and pans until they shine.

Doing the dishes is an excellent everyday opportunity for deepening intimacy with your loved ones. Share the task and experience the synergy—and energy—that comes from teamwork. Teenagers often open up more about their lives when they are occupied with a task than when they are put on the spot. Cleaning up time can be a time for silence and mediation, or laughter and sharing. You do the dishes every day, and by using the power of choice, you can have it be a task that gives you energy instead of depletes you. However you approach it, you will soon quit dreading doing the dishes—you may even look forward to it!

꙳ ꙳ ꙳ ꙳ ꙳ ꙳ ꙳ ꙳ ꙳

ALTER Your Dishwashing

꙳ ꙳ ꙳ ꙳ ꙳ ꙳ ꙳

ASK YOURSELF:

How do I experience washing the dishes?

Do I choose to make dishwashing a
spiritually rewarding experience?

Do I experience dishwashing
as the conclusion of my feast?

TELL YOURSELF:

"Humility and simplicity renew me."

GIVE YOURSELF:

- an attitude of gratitude for each moment of
your life

- a dishwashing partner to share your trials and
blessings

- an inspirational plaque by the sink with a
saying you love

Living an Intentional Life

Opportunity Knocks

WHATEVER OPPORTUNITIES APPEAR in your life—great or small—you are equipped to deal with them when you are committed to live an intentional life. Over time, your commitment to awareness, your choices and intention will prepare you for a life beyond your greatest expectations. Over time, an astonishing transformation occurs in your mind, body and soul. Your life not only becomes more meaningful, but you may discover a new purpose for your life that you were never aware of before.

His Holiness

Another of my beloved mentors has been His Holiness the fourteenth Dalai Lama. I have had the honor to study with His Holiness and experience his wisdom, humor and love. It is impossible to sit in his presence and not be in awe of the manner in which he lives an intentional life.

As a young man, His Holiness witnessed the unimaginable slaughter and horrors of the Communist takeover of his homeland of Tibet. Scores of his loved ones were killed, and he barely escaped with his own life. Through it all, he continued to surrender to what life brought before him and practiced peace, awareness and compassion—practices that were second nature to him because they were woven into the very fabric of his everyday life. Those practices gave him the power to face challenges most would collapse in the face of; they gave him the courage that comes from knowing who he was deep down inside, and the wisdom to make choices based on his deepest convictions. No matter how life has challenged him, he sees potential, love, and possibility in the experience.

Over the last fifty years His Holiness has evolved from being an obscure spiritual leader in a remote mountainous region to an inspirational global figure who continues to give our troubled planet hope for the future. He turned the destructive energy of genocide and exile into the constructive energy of a worldwide movement for peace. In a world embroiled in greed, oppression, and violence, he models and teaches peace, love, nonviolence, forgiveness and compassion. No matter what challenges life brings him, he sees potential, love and possibility in every experience.

His Holiness the Dalai Lama views his seemingly horrible exile as a blessing, as the world now knows more about Buddhism because of his abrupt entry into the international arena. He has become a highly visible spokesperson for and incarnation of the tenets of Buddha and a visionary who holds to his dream of a world based on reverence for all living beings. By committing to living an intentional life by living his firm convictions, he has unleashed a personal power that makes him the world leader he is today.

Why did I choose this particular story when talking about how to live an intentional life? When you first become aware that there is an opportunity to live in a new way, for the rest of your life, a choice immediately emerges. The choice may become clear. The question arises: Can I surrender to something new, and in that surrender experience my life as infinite possibilities? Or, do I continue to orchestrate and direct my life to include what I want to experience and isolate any experience that may tax me or make me feel uncomfortable?

If you choose to live an intentional life of infinite possibilities, then you have chosen the road less traveled. When you choose this path, it is important to underpin your life with spiritual practices to give you strength and courage for your journey. Without exception, all of the extraordinary people that have contributed to my life—Jimmy Carter, Desmond Tutu, the Dalai Lama, Thich Nhat Hanh, Mother Teresa, and so many more—all maintain daily spiritual practices. They keep themselves ready for the bumps in the road of life. Their greatness has evolved from their simple daily practices.

There is an old saying that goes something like this: "The person who prizes the smallest things in life is surely worthy of the great ones." I promise you this: as you practice acts of awareness, live mindfully, and experience new choices available to you, you will experience the fruits of living an intentional life. This is the reward of embracing an intentional life: full participation in the world on many levels: emotional, physical, intellectual and spiritual.

CHAPTER NINETEEN

The Evening News

꙳ ꙳ ꙳ ꙳ ꙳ ꙳ ꙳ ꙳ ꙳ ꙳

"Current events are so grim that we often can't decide
whether or not we dare to watch the six o'clock news."

~Anonymous

꙳ ꙳ ꙳ ꙳ ꙳ ꙳ ꙳

HAVE YOU STOPPED WATCHING the evening news? A great number of people in America have decided not to watch the news anymore. There are a variety of reasons given by people for not watching the news, but you shouldn't stop. Choose to watch the news in order to stay informed about what is happening in our world. Watch the news, just do it in a different way.

One of the biggest challenges we face in modern times is finding a way to maintain some semblance of inner calm while staying informed about world events. It is important to remember that, as with everything, we have a *choice* in the way we respond to this constant parade of catastrophes and fears.

Some of us choose to reject the daily news and live in anger. Others accept it and live in fear. And some of us deny that they have any power at all in the matter. Others of us bring the seemingly daily disasters of our modern world so deeply into our minds and souls that it profoundly interferes with the quality of our lives. But just as we choose anger, fear, helplessness, and distress, we can also choose serenity, compassion, commitment, and wisdom.

The End is Not Near

Since man has been able to speak, he has been proclaiming that the end of the world is right around the corner. Every ten years or so, one of Nostradamus's predictions surfaces, signaling that it is time for us all to dive under our beds. The Y2K frenzy created a multi-million dollar industry in books, seminars, and supplies to prepare us for the end of the world. Armageddon peddlers play on people's fears based on the idea of the "in group," the "out group," and the "chosen ones." Fear is traded as a commodity and exploited as a political strategy. It's unsettling that a select few have created this mythical frenzy and cashed in on fortunes through manipulating the human psyche.

Still, whatever our particular political viewpoint, we all seem to be in agreement that these are serious times. Whether it is the scarcity of drinkable water, the melting of the polar icecaps, or the constant threat of terrorism, the overall response is: "What's the world coming to?" The stakes have never seemed so high, and it feels as though our country—and our world—is at a crossroads. Now more than ever it is important that we remain mindful of which road we are choosing to walk down in the everyday choices that make up the fabric of our lives.

No One's Left Behind

How can you keep current events from dampening your spirits? How can you watch the news without being trapped in a web of doom?

Begin by watching the news objectively. Be aware of catch phrases, listen for charged words, watch the manipulation of language. Discern whether the news is based on reality or sensationalism. Assess your news "habits": do you listen to the news actively, or passively? Do you choose your new sources consciously, or unconsciously? What emotions do you feel as you listen to the news? What thoughts? You can develop your own mindfulness practices that will soon be second nature and keep you from being negatively affected by the news.

Gather the facts, from different sources when possible, detach yourself from them, and practice compassion for those involved. When you hear of a horrible accident or a convenience store robbery, practice compassion for all the people involved—the victims, the police and emergency personnel, even the perpetrators who will be held responsible for their actions. If you pray, put the people concerned in the news story on your prayer list, or spend a few moments mindfully sending them healing thoughts.

Instead of being victimized by the event, choose to tap into the amazing power of commitment. An old axiom goes: "If you are not part of the solution, you are part of the problem." Whether it's the welfare of our animal friends, the health of our forests, or a deeper level of communication with our fellow humans around the globe, your heart will tell you which path to take.

Amidst all the noise of the modern media, make time to listen to that still quiet voice within. Then mindfully choose the way you interpret the evening news. Living intentionally means being aware of what creates passion within you, and putting your energy into that specific area. Don't allow yourself to be distracted or defeated. Our feelings of powerlessness stem from doing nothing, so focus on a project, no matter how small, that warms your heart and makes the world a slightly better place. It could be as simple as visiting an elderly neighbor or as challenging as running for office. When you participate in the world around you, you become part of the solution that heals the plague of apathy in our country.

⚹ ⚹ ⚹ ⚹ ⚹ ⚹ ⚹ ⚹ ⚹ ⚹

ALTER Your Evening News

⚹ ⚹ ⚹ ⚹ ⚹ ⚹ ⚹

ASK YOURSELF:

What are my current sources of news?

Why do I choose this particular news source?

How does watching the evening news affect my life?"

TELL YOURSELF:

"I have power in our world."

GIVE YOURSELF:

- an online subscription to a magazine or newspaper from another country

- a new news source once a week

- a notepad by the television to create a prayer/concern list as you watch the news

CHAPTER TWENTY

Family

❀ ❀ ❀ ❀ ❀ ❀ ❀ ❀ ❀

*The greatest institution in the world
is the human family.*

~Anonymous

❀ ❀ ❀ ❀ ❀ ❀ ❀

COMMUNITY IS A GIFT from the Divine. Nothing has greater impact on our well-being than love and relationships. The University of Michigan published a landmark paper that demonstrated people without strong social support were two to four times more likely to die than those with substantial social networks.

Television shows often serve as surrogate families for old and young alike. TV's *Late Night with David Letterman Show* and others like it are consciously designed as family models with the father, the son, the wacky uncle all playing their parts. This structure is something we are familiar and comfortable with.

The family is the first and most profound layer of social relationships in our lives. It is where we learn to connect, communicate, and commit.

A New View of Family

The Donna Reed Show and *Leave It to Beaver* were historical television representations of family. This experience of family was rigid, static, boxed within the suburbanization of the country. There is now fluidity in family. We now have *Friends* and *Will & Grace* redefining our modern notions of family, teaching us that in addition to our biological families, we can form supportive networks of relationships that meet our authentic needs for love and intimacy.

A family can best be defined as a primary social group that shares the same gene pool, or shares common beliefs, or activities. We don't have to constrict ourselves to the traditional model of mom, dad, and kids. Family doesn't even necessarily have to be in the same location. By maintaining close relationships and regular contact, we can create a family.

Family has an extended definition and the family image is constantly changing. Family is a dynamic idea, not a static model, that we are continuously redefining because we have to.

While we may believe that this flexible idea of the family is new, in fact it is not. The founders of major religions displayed this in their lives. Christ, Buddha, Mohammad, Moses, all created families of disciples and followers.

The concept of the family has now expanded to the notion of one human family. One of the greatest reminders and reinforcements of this idea is the horror of 9/11 and how all people—stockbrokers, rescue workers, janitors—joined together as a global family in the face of crisis. Hopefully, what we have learned from the 9/11 tragedy, is that we can reach out and create families anywhere, anytime, any place.

I'll Be There for You

Kendall Hailey observes, "The great gift of family life is to be intimately acquainted with people you might have never even introduced yourself to had life not done it for you." Our family of origin is an incredible gift. A family can be the most fertile place for spiritual development. Families are the container, the vehicle, the petri dish for our growth potential. Inside the family people experience the raw vulnerability of you. Therein lies its power.

We also have the privilege and the ability to choose families. Look for opportunities to create families in your life, as they are all around you. Create a family around a book club, a project, the military, an association, a cause, a religious group. Even if you live alone, you have the potential to create your own family with animals, plants, neighbors, and friends. Re-vision your workplace as "one big family" and see if it doesn't improve your day to day experiences on the job.

⅍ ⅍ ⅍ ⅍ ⅍ ⅍ ⅍ ⅍ ⅍ ⅍

ALTER Your Family

⅍ ⅍ ⅍ ⅍ ⅍ ⅍ ⅍

ASK YOURSELF:

What do I think of when I hear the word "family"?

Who do I consider to be my family?

Am I willing to extend my definition of family?

TELL YOURSELF:

"I am a member of our one human family."

GIVE YOURSELF:

- many different families: at home, work, in the neighborhood, book club, meditation group, or church

- mementos of loved ones around you

- The choice to create new families

CHAPTER TWENTY-ONE

Intimacy

᪗ ᪗ ᪗ ᪗ ᪗ ᪗ ᪗ ᪗ ᪗ ᪗

*We can be intimate with flowers, animals, trees, and stars,
and can be nourished by the experience. But the most
powerful and profound awareness of ourselves occurs with
our simultaneous opening up with another human.*

~Pat Malone

᪗ ᪗ ᪗ ᪗ ᪗ ᪗ ᪗

WHAT DO YOU THINK when you hear the word "intimacy"? You may pause and listen more intensely. You may look with an eye of suspicion. Or like many of us, you may sigh with a feeling of being overwhelmed—just one more thing to do.

If you ask a hundred people the definition of intimacy, the majority would link intimacy with sexual behavior. Let's challenge ourselves to expand the definition of intimacy beyond the sexual context. Instead let's consider intimacy as closeness, familiarity, affection, understanding, and connection—not exclusively with others, but with ourselves primarily. Intimacy with ourselves is a significant and important first step, for it is impossible to have intimacy with another person if we don't have it with ourselves first.

Intimacy is primarily how you see into yourself. Secondarily, it is how others experience you. It is an act of great courage to intentionally want to see who you really are. It requires vulnerability and surrender to achieve intimacy. When you give yourself permission to see into yourself, what you discover may allow you a deeper, more profound connection with yourself, with the Divine, and with others.

Intimacy, like food and shelter, is one of our basic human needs.

Intimacy Heals

A host of scientific studies correlate intimacy with health. According to Dr. Dean Ornish, "Love and intimacy are at the root of what makes us sick and what makes us well; what causes sadness, and what brings happiness; what makes us suffer, and what leads to healing. If a new drug had the same impact, virtually every doctor in the country would be recommending it to their patients. It would be malpractice not to prescribe it."

What is stopping you from experiencing intimacy? Past difficulties in relationships and the resulting fear, anger, or depression can cause disconnections in our current relationships with ourselves and others. We tend to withdraw, and a numbness develops in our bodies and souls to the point where intimacy may seem impossible.

Sleep deprivation or insomnia can also inhibit intimacy. When we are exhausted, it is almost impossible to muster the energy to be intimate. Stress—a modern epidemic—creates a state of almost constant worry and defensiveness within us. We worry about what happened yesterday and what will happen tomorrow. When we rob ourselves of the present moment, there is no possibility for intimacy, for intimacy only happens when you can be fully aware and deepen the "now" you are experiencing with your loved one.

Cell phones, e-mails, and beepers often serve to isolate and alienate us even more while giving only an illusion of intimacy, as we are not physically in the presence of another person. Our current culture dictates that we move faster, move forward, reach outward for some sort of fantasy of fulfillment in the material world. But true intimacy is a slowing down, a moving inward, a spiral journey toward your authentic self.

Intentional Intimacy

Many of us are disconnected, absent and truly not present in the rush of our lives. We are distracted, preoccupied and exhausted. The journey back to our intimate self is not an event, it is a process that takes intention and commitment. If intimacy has been missing from your life for a long time, it won't return overnight. Intimacy is like a muscle that needs to be exercised and cared for on a regular basis or it will atrophy.

Intimacy is an opening of the heart. Intimacy is moving toward yourself, your environment, or another in openness, acceptance, and reverence, not a moving away in fear, judgment, and condemnation. You can experience intimacy not only with others, but with yourself, animals, nature . . . anything in your environment.

The primary practice to employ to reach intimacy is awareness. Turn off the distractions: radios, televisions, computers, cell phones, beepers. All of these wonderful technological tools create motion, movement, excitement and distraction in our souls. Imagine this as an adventure into the full, vulnerable, sensual, creative you.

At any given moment in our lives, we are either moving toward greater intimacy with ourselves, our environment, and our loved ones, or we are pulling back from intimacy. Explore intimacy through your senses; smells, touch, sounds, tastes, images. Begin with nature. If you love the ocean, imagine the ocean breeze on the skin of your body, the smell and feel of salt. Experience the thrill and awe of the sunset or the sunrise over the water.

You may enjoy rain more. As the rain surrounds you, imagine the smell, the sound, the feel. There are innumerable possibilities to experience a primal sense of intimacy in nature: the silence of a fresh snow; a summer night echoing with the sound of crickets; or the midnight sky scattered with bright stars. Nature is a powerful ally on your path to intimacy.

Animals are also a profound source of intimacy. They consistently gift us with love and faithful companionship. If you have lost touch with your intimate self, try lying down beside your dog or cat and in the silence be aware of the connection between you and the animal. The natural intimacy of animals calls us to mirror them and become intimate ourselves.

There is nothing like a great book to transport you to another time and place, where you can undergo a myriad of emotions and relationships within the pages at your fingertips. Sitting on the back porch wrapped in a down comforter, you can experience intimacy with yourself, with the characters, with the scenes of your book.

When you find yourself becoming numb or lost, why not try pulling out your favorite movie? Discover movies you love that lead you home to yourself. A good movie can be like a trusted friend.

Finally, develop your own sacred intimate practices. Create rituals that make you feel loved, nurtured, and appreciated. Try designing your own tea ceremony, a sensual bath, or a restorative nap. There are many doors that are available to you to open and see into your self. There are many windows to the soul. Nature, water, music, art, a pet—all of these have the potential for engaging the senses and thus creating a greater intimacy with yourself and others.

While not exclusive to intimacy, if you feel that depression, anxiety or insomnia are keeping you from intimacy or limiting you in any other way from fully experiencing your life, you may want to explore meditation, prayer, yoga, or other mindfulness exercises. If these practices do not help you with your depression, anxiety, or insomnia, you may want to consult a physician. There are remarkable medicines available on the market today that are helping people live healthier, more productive lives. You can try different methods to help yourself or ask a professional for help, but there is no reason for you to suffer.

Intimacy, in all its many forms, is a part of your life. Intimacy should not be quantified by a specific time, with a specific person, at a specific place. True, authentic intimacy can be experienced in your everyday activities.

༝ ༝ ༝ ༝ ༝ ༝ ༝ ༝ ༝ ༝

ALTER Your Intimacy

༝ ༝ ༝ ༝ ༝ ༝ ༝

ASK YOURSELF:

Right now, in this moment, am I moving
toward intimacy or away from it?

In what ways do I experience intimacy?

How can I deepen my intimacy with myself and my loved ones?

TELL YOURSELF:

"I am perfect, whole, and complete."

GIVE YOURSELF:

- time alone in nature

- a strong commitment to unstructured time
  with your loved ones

- a journal to keep a chronicle of your path to
  greater intimacy

CHAPTER TWENTY-TWO

Bath

ৡ ৡ ৡ ৡ ৡ ৡ ৡ ৡ ৡ ৡ

There is no need to go to India or anywhere else to find
peace. You will find that deep place of silence right in
your room, your garden, or even your bathtub.

~Elizabeth Kubler-Ross

ৡ ৡ ৡ ৡ ৡ ৡ ৡ

N OUR FAST-PACED WORLD, the bath has become an
oasis for the mind, body and soul. There has been a great
revival in discovering ways to relax and nestle in our homes
and the bath has emerged as a primary focus. Americans spend
more money building and renovating bathrooms than they do
on any other room in the house. The size of our bedrooms is
staying the same, but the size of our bathrooms is growing. This
shows our profound desire for to seek nurturing and serenity.
While we appreciate the bath in Western culture, we have largely
lost the deeper meaning and spiritual connection with the art
of bathing.

A study from the Sleep Disorders Clinic at Stanford University
found bathing helpful in the treatment of sleep disorders. When
your body gets ready for sleep, your body temperature drops. A
bath reduces your body temperature and nudges your bedtime

biochemistry along. In 2000, a Harris Interactive poll found that 100 percent of the 2,000 women interviewed found baths relaxing. Sixty percent said they would be happier if they could take a bath every day.

We use pictures of delighted children playing in the bathtub for greeting cards, calendars, and gifts. We remember bathing as babies and kids. We remember the bath being a playful time, a time of giggling and spontaneity. We were thrilled with our nakedness, the comfort of our bodies.

Communion

The bath physically embodies the idea of "sanctuary." The bath is a sacred relaxation ritual. We need to concentrate more on the experience, and less on the function, of the bath. We need to make the time for a real bath.

The central art of bathing underpins many cultures. In Roman times, lounging around baths was a day-to-day element of their culture. In Japan, communal baths are a social event. Baths have traditionally been used for medicinal purposes as well. U.S. President Franklin D. Roosevelt used the natural warm springs near his summer home in Georgia as a treatment for his polio. Both ancient and modern, as well as conventional and alternative healers prescribe baths using herbs, salts, and oils for treating a wide array of disorders.

Water has always symbolized purification and release in all spiritualities and religious traditions: for Christians, baptism;

for Hindus, purification in the River Ganges; for Jews, *mikva*, a communal bath for ritual cleansing; for Muslims, *wudu*, the ritual washing that must take place before prayer. Whatever the intent, it is evident that the bath is a significant part of our history.

Renewal

A bath is never ordinary. Baths are different every day of your life because you are different every day of your life. Change one element: aromatherapy, candles, soap, music, silence. Use what you need for that particular bath to make it unique. Take a bath in candlelight or completely in the dark. Start at the top of your head and work to your toes relaxing yourself in the water. Run a bubble bath and play sculptor with the foam.

The bath is also a great place to meditate and do guided imagery. You can let your mind take you to any place in the universe. What a wonderful gift to combine the healing power of the bath with the healing power of guided imagery.

The bath is an act of re-membering and re-creation. *Remember* the waters of your mother's womb. *Recreate* what you need today. *Release* by writing words in the water connected to any experience or emotion you want to release from your body or soul. These words take presence in the water. As you open the drain, imagine the words swirling down the drain. *Reclaim* who you are, uncluttered, focused, and new.

ꚺ ꚺ ꚺ ꚺ ꚺ ꚺ ꚺ ꚺ ꚺ ꚺ

ALTER Your Bath

ꚺ ꚺ ꚺ ꚺ ꚺ ꚺ ꚺ

ASK YOURSELF:

Do I want to take more baths?

Can I choose to schedule a regular bath?

What are my memories of the bath?

TELL YOURSELF:

"I relax into the water."

GIVE YOURSELF:

• aromatherapy bath salts

• candles for the bath area

• a beautiful print or painting on the wall by the bath

CHAPTER TWENTY-THREE

Quiet Time, Meditation, and Prayer

༈ ༈ ༈ ༈ ༈ ༈ ༈ ༈ ༈ ༈

Every major religion has referred to inner guidance in its
teachings . . . the Spirit of Christ, the Atman, God within . . .

~Christine M. Comstock

༈ ༈ ༈ ༈ ༈ ༈ ༈

MEDITATION AND PRAYER make us aware of the presence of God. There are many paths into that Divine presence. Human beings have spent centuries and lifetimes exploring avenues to get closer to God. Each of us wants the full experience of Divine love, acceptance, and communion. We have attempted this within ourselves and across cultures with many types of prayers and meditations.

Meditation has a powerful effect on our health. The federal government's new Office of Alternative Medicine reports that for over 25 years Dr. Herbert Benson at Harvard has created a large body of research on the science of meditation. According to decades of research, people who meditate have significantly fewer migraine headaches, their anxiety and depression levels drop remarkably, and they miss fewer days at work. Most patients with high blood pressure recover completely, or at least improve, and 75 percent of insomniacs are cured and 25 percent improve.

Many convincing studies also demonstrate the amazing effect prayer has on healing. Dr. Larry Dossey cites hundreds of studies that verify the effectiveness of prayer in the healing process. Cardiologist Randolph Byrd at San Francisco General Hospital took 393 patients admitted to the coronary care unit and divided them into two groups. One group had 192 patients that were prayed for by home prayer groups of five to seven people. The second group was 201 patients that were not remembered in prayer. The study was conducted with strict criteria. Neither the doctors, nurses, nor patients, knew which group individual patients were in. The study concluded the prayed-for patients were five times less likely than the non-prayed-for group to require antibiotics. They were three times less likely to develop pulmonary edema. None of the prayed-for patients needed endotracheal intubations. And fewer patients in the prayed-for group died.

Catherine of Sienna wrote: "Perfect prayer is achieved, not with many words, but with loving desire. Everything you do can be a prayer." Prayer has usually been taught as a discipline that must be learned, but nothing could be further from the truth. Prayer is as natural as our breathing. It is natural for us to want to be in a relationship with the Divine. It merely takes having the intention to be aware of the Divine presence in all things.

There are many manners of prayer. A prayer of petition asks for something for one's self. Intercessory prayer asks for something for others—be it healing, forgiveness, or guidance. We offer gratitude in a prayer of thanksgiving. Centering prayer—an ancient form of Christian contemplative prayer—involves entering silence and listening to God. The examen, or the examination of conscience, is a type of prayer where we conduct a moral inventory of our lives, examining ourselves, and thereby developing an honesty with ourselves and with God. The final stage of the prayer of examen is asking for forgiveness. The types of prayer shift within traditions and continue to evolve as we learn and grow.

Cycles of Prayer

As varied as the types of prayer are the cycles of prayer. We have annual cycles of prayer that differ according to spiritual and religious traditions. For Christians, the Lenten prayers are prayers of forgiveness. For Jews, the prayers of Yom Kippur are prayers of repentance. For Muslims, the prayers of Ramadan are prayers of sacrifice and devotion. Different traditions have daily cycles of prayer. Muslims are required by the practice of *Salat* to pray five times a day. Jews pray three times daily, each time designated by one of the founders of the faith. Christians are reminded to pray upon waking, before meals, and before going to sleep.

Religions have developed not only many methods for prayer, but also many aids to assist us in the practice of prayer. Many spiritual practitioners use prayer beads, which are found in almost every major religion. Prayer rugs are used in Islam to keep the site of prayer free from dirt of any sort. Prayer flags are used by Tibetan Buddhists to carry prayers and blessings to all the people in the path of the wind. Icons—painted images of Christ or holy people—are physical objects to help connect the prayerful to God. *Mezuzahs* hold a prayer of blessing at the door of the Jewish home.

How to Pray

Prayer is the most personal and intimate of all spiritual practices. Different types of prayer resonate with different types of people. Explore different methods of prayer for yourself. In the centering prayer—the ancient practice of contemplation—you sit in a quite place, focus on your breath, and then repeat one word or a small phrase over and over, eventually experiencing communion with God. Many people prefer a memorized prayer like the Christian "The Lord's Prayer." You can also pray with holy scriptures. Meditation practices vary as well, but the most basic form is going into silence and listening.

Prayer is about first becoming aware then discovering God in that awareness. A saint from the early Christian church told this story:

"Help us find God," the disciples asked the elder.

"No one can help you do that," the elder said.

"Why not?" the disciples asked, amazed.

"For the same reason that no one can help fish to find the ocean."

꙳ ꙳ ꙳ ꙳ ꙳ ꙳ ꙳ ꙳ ꙳ ꙳

ALTER Your Quiet Time

꙳ ꙳ ꙳ ꙳ ꙳ ꙳ ꙳

ASK YOURSELF:

Am I satisfied in my practice of meditation and prayer?

What would I choose to change about
my meditations and prayers?

What is keeping me from practicing
meditation and prayer as I would like?

TELL YOURSELF:

"In the silence I experience rebirth."

GIVE YOURSELF:

- 10-20 minutes of meditation/prayer a day

- a special place in your home for meditation/
prayer

- a cushion, mat, prayer beads or prayer shawl to
enhance your practice of meditation/prayer

CHAPTER TWENTY-FOUR

Sleeping

❦ ❦ ❦ ❦ ❦ ❦ ❦ ❦ ❦ ❦

Blessings on him that first invented sleep! It covers a man thoughts and all, like a cloak; it is meat for the hungry, drink for the thirsty, heat for the cold, and cold for the hot. It is the current coin that purchases cheaply all the pleasures of the world, and the balance that sets even king and shepherd, fool and sage.

~Cervantes

❦ ❦ ❦ ❦ ❦ ❦ ❦

OUR NATION IS IN DANGER because of our lack of reverence for sleep. Sleep is a necessity, not a luxury, yet over 100 million Americans are sleep deprived. Sleep is a naturally occurring cycle that we need to respect, not control. Just as the seasons and other aspects of nature manifest cycles, sleep is a natural, cyclical event that we must honor.

With the advent of late night shows, thousands of channels to surf, all-night social events, even round-the-clock, fully-lit sporting venues, we are overstimulated with light, sound, and action. Traditionally the hour or two before sleep has been dimly lit and low-key. Staring into a lit screen for many hours makes your brain think it is daytime, and can give you trouble going to sleep.

Sleep Science

Many Americans are running on six hours of sleep or less. We take sleeping pills at night and reach for stimulants such as caffeine first thing in the morning in an effort to control our natural cycles. But the body has a wisdom of its own, and will answer our attempts to force it into unnatural patterns with mild to severe physical and mental disorders. You can have significant mood shifts, including depression and increased irritability. You may lose coping skills.

The anxiety of sleep deprivation can cause you to overeat to soothe yourself, resulting in weight gain. Over-the-counter sleeping pills are one of the fastest growing categories of medicine. Insomnia has become an epidemic. Still, people do not want to go to their doctors about this problem. Sleep aids may offer a temporary fix, but they are not solving the problem, as they do not treat the underlying cause. Treating the physiological component won't work especially if there is a spiritual problem. The precise function of sleep remains a mystery, but as we spend one third of our lives sleeping doesn't it deserve our respect?

Without sleep, your body's immune cells don't function. Consequently, your immunity to infections and disease is reduced. Your productivity is reduced because your cognitive functioning is impaired. Approximately one-third of all drivers have fallen asleep at some point while driving a car.

We must have sleep: It is a matter of life and death. Our bodies must have deep, REM sleep to function. We must dream to maintain our emotional, physical, and spiritual health. You can very literally go insane without REM sleep. What's more, restorative sleep is an essential component of living an intentional life.

Sweet Dreams

Consciously reconnect with the renewing and replenishing power of sleep. Every system in your body is refreshed and restored each time you sleep. Healing occurs during our sleep cycles, so when you are ill or run down, honor your body's needs for more sleep.

Listen to your body. Your body will tell you how much sleep you need. Practice awareness and respect the messages your body sends you. Don't try to force it into an artificial pattern that causes you to be chronically overtired. We have a seriously damaging cultural myth that people who sleep fewer hours are more productive and in some way more "successful," when in fact the opposite is really true. Well-rested people are more focused and efficient than the sleep-deprived.

Practicing awareness tends to your soul's needs. Imagine sleep as grace. Surrender. Allow yourself to be enveloped with sleep's grace, in its abundance, in its caring and healing nature.

Create a sanctuary in your bedroom; make a reverent space that honors sleep for the sacred healing experience it is. Be rigorous about reserving that space for quiet activities such as reading, for physical intimacy, and most of all, for sweet dreams.

Invest in your bedroom by adding peaceful colors, a good mattress, nice sheets, a comfortable pillow: after all, you spend a third of your life there.

ᴥ ᴥ ᴥ ᴥ ᴥ ᴥ ᴥ ᴥ ᴥ ᴥ

ALTER Your Sleep

ᴥ ᴥ ᴥ ᴥ ᴥ ᴥ ᴥ

ASK YOURSELF:

What is my current bedtime ritual? Does it
enhance the quality of my sleep?

How much sleep do I need to feel refreshed each day?

If I am sleep deprived, am I ready to change my habits?

TELL YOURSELF:

"A magnificent healing process occurs within me as I sleep."

GIVE YOURSELF:

- a bedroom makeover that focuses on creating
  a nurturing, peaceful environment

- a warm bath before retiring

- a "media curfew" one half hour before bedtime

A Bird Named Goober

I **WAS WAITING FOR A TABLE** at The Flying Biscuit, a popular restaurant in Atlanta that I often frequent. I was number thirty in line and the hostess had just called out number five. My daughter phoned to say she was stuck in traffic. Frustrated, with unexpected time on my hands, I wandered down the street. All of a sudden, the sky darkened and buckets of rain poured down. I ducked into a little gift shop.

It was an adorable shop filled with pottery and unusual gifts. Stewing over an afternoon gone wrong, I browsed around with little interest, occasionally picking something up and putting it down.

Then something screeched. I looked around but didn't see anything.

I picked up a china teapot and high-pitched screeching rang through the shop again. A shopkeeper unpacking some pottery by the cash register seemed unaffected by the weird noise. I approached the woman and looked behind the counter.

On the floor sat an old birdcage with a fragile little bird inside gazing up at me. The shopkeeper walked over and lifted the cage onto the counter.

She smiled and said, "This is Goober. He's crying because it's lunchtime." As she opened the cage, she said, "Don't worry. He can't fly away. His wing is broken."

She then opened a small plastic container and picked up a single chopstick. She picked up a tiny bit of food with the chopstick and continued talking as she slowly and reverently fed the weak little creature.

"People race up and down the road outside. They hit these little birds all the time—sometimes a cat or a dog. I don't have much money. And I have a few health problems myself. But this is something good I can do in the world. No one else seems to care about these little critters. But to me they are all really tiny angels sent here to love us."

I was deeply moved by the tenderness with which she fed Goober, almost as though she were performing a sacred ritual, with great mindfulness and reverence. I watched in amazement, humbled to be in the presence of the woman and her pet. She explained to me that each night, with arthritic hands, she cuts, peels, mashes, and then (with great intention, I was sure) mixes grapes, seeds, and honey for the birds she rescues. She believed that her love and devotion goes into the little bird's food, and that will help him get better.

I was awed by her reverence: by her awareness of this small, ordinary animal. Mother Teresa was surely right when she said, "We can do no great things, only small things with great love."

This beautiful woman had, with awareness, choice and intention, rescued tiny creatures that many others don't see or don't care about. The ripple effect of the great care and reverence she brought to Goober's lunchtime nourished and healed more than just Goober.

So, wherever you are, begin with great love in your heart and a small thing in your life. You may not stumble over the Divine, but you can discover it in surprising places, in fleeting moments, in the simplest of ways. It can be found every day, and transformation is the reward.

What is holding you back from living a meaningful and intentional life? Are you ready to confront, as Thoreau put it, "the essential facts of life?"

For me, a dirty bathroom was an opportunity to move beyond judgment and rage. Removing a dead dog from the road taught me reverence and respect for all God's creations. Experiencing political defeat offered lessons in humility, love and in the healing transformational power of community.

I hope this book has helped you discover the many opportunities that await you in your everyday life as you choose to live an intentional life. Before long, the idea of living beyond your comfort zone will be welcomed, not feared. Paths less traveled will provide the deep sense of satisfaction and peace of mind you crave in our complex, noisy, and careless modern world.

Any misfortune might call forth the courage and compassion that has been long hidden within you. But your own journey doesn't have to begin with dramatic events. You can do it, not through ritual or dogma or elaborate schemes, but merely through awareness, your choices and your commitment to live an intentional life.

ABOUT THE AUTHOR

One of the nation's leading authorities on stress management, wellness and work-life balance, Dr. Kathleen Hall, founder and CEO of Alter Your Life, is the leader of the Intentional Life movement. As an author, speaker and stress-management expert, Dr. Hall teaches individuals and corporations how to Live an Intentional Life of purpose, health and balance. Her own life serves  as a testimony to achieving a life of deeper fulfillment and well-being. Dr. Hall left her life as a financial advisor with a Wall Street firm at the World Trade Center, and made a radical choice to redefine success on her own terms. She has studied with some of the greatest spiritual and medical leaders of our time including President Jimmy Carter, the Dalai Lama, Bishop Desmond Tutu, Dr. Dean Ornish of the Preventive Medicine Research Institute, and Dr. Herbert Benson at the Harvard Mind-Body Institute. She regularly contributes to national print, radio, and television media including CNN, *Fortune, Time, Cosmopolitan, USA Today* and *The Wall Street Journal* and has presented to corporations including The Home Depot and Office Depot.

Dr. Hall earned a B.S in Finance from Jacksonville State University, an M. Div. from Emory University, and a Doctorate in Spirituality from Columbia Theological Seminary, and has clinical training from Harvard University. She lives on her ranch with her family and a variety of rescue animals in Clarkesville, Georgia. Dr. Hall can be found at www.drkathleenhall.com and www.alteryourlife.com.